Quarterly Essay

Quarterly Essay is published four times a year by Black Inc., an imprint of Schwartz Books Pty Ltd. Publisher: Morry Schwartz.

ISBN 9781760644383 ISSN 1444-884x

Subscriptions – 1 year print & digital (4 issues): $89.99 within Australia incl. GST. Outside Australia $124.99. 2 years print & digital (8 issues): $169.99 within Australia incl. GST. 1 year digital only: $59.99.

Payment may be made by Mastercard or Visa, or by cheque made out to Schwartz Books. Payment includes postage and handling.

To subscribe, fill out and post the subscription card or form inside this issue, or subscribe online:

quarterlyessay.com
subscribe@quarterlyessay.com
Phone: 61 3 9486 0288

Correspondence should be addressed to:

The Editor, Quarterly Essay
22–24 Northumberland Street
Collingwood VIC 3066 Australia
Phone: 61 3 9486 0288 / Fax: 61 3 9011 6106
Email: quarterlyessay@blackincbooks.com

Editor: Chris Feik. Management: Elisabeth Young. Publicity: Anna Lensky. Design: Guy Mirabella. Associate Editor: Kirstie Innes-Will. Production Coordinator: Marilyn de Castro. Typesetting: Typography Studio.

Printed in Australia by McPherson's Printing Group. The paper used to produce this book comes from wood grown in sustainable forests.

"Time is a flat circle. Everything we've ever done or will ever do, we're gonna do over and over and over again."

True Detective, Season 1

"The thing about the old days: they the old days."

The Wire, Season 4

BAD COP

Peter Dutton's strongman politics

Lech Blaine

Peter Dutton eats bleeding-heart lefties for breakfast. He is tall and bald, with a resting death stare. His eyes – two brown beads – see evil so that the weak can be blind. His lips are allergic to political correctness. Peter preaches the gospel of John Howard with the fanaticism of Paul Keating. He wants to do the Labor Party slowly, slowly, slowly, and defeat the woe-is-me heroism of identity politics.

"It's a movement that seeks to define and divide us by class, sex, race, religion and more besides," said Dutton in 2023. "Worse, such movements seek to undermine traditional values of ambition, gratitude and forgiveness and replace them with resentment, envy and anger."

Once upon a time, the federal Opposition leader was a cop in clammy Queensland. He was a listener, a lurker, a watcher; not a storyteller, nor a performer. He set traps for suspects and waited for them to make a mistake. For poker-faced Dutton, leadership isn't about kissing the cheeks of babies, or the arses of journalists. It is about bleeding for your beliefs and denying the griefs of your enemies. White lies are often the cost of beating the bad guys. "In a different age, we'd be clashing swords," Dutton told journalist Madonna King in 2014. "I see myself as a contestant in that battle."

In May 2022, Australia just so happened to elect a good cop as prime minister. Anthony Albanese promised a cuddlier, less bloodthirsty form of leadership. "Safe change," with a patient embrace of democratic rituals. He got a two-seat majority on the basis of not being Scott Morrison. Labor gained nine seats, and lost one to the Greens. The Liberal party room bled seventeen members. A coup had been staged in six of the Liberals' most blue-chip seats by teal independents. Professional women in inner-city seats had been forsaken in the Coalition's pursuit of materialistic, politically incorrect men.

After Morrison, there was only one serious contender left standing: Peter Dutton. If the Liberals hadn't lost six seats to the teal independents, Josh Frydenberg was the obvious next Opposition leader. At the very least, he would have been waiting in the wings to replace Dutton. The 2022 election erased Frydenberg as a direct leadership rival. And it removed a posse of moderate MPs who would have agitated against Dutton's vision for where the Liberal Party should be heading politically. "I grew up in a working-class suburb with two loving parents who were hard-working small business people," said Dutton in his acceptance speech.

Dutton's ascension showed how the Liberal Party had changed, both electorally and culturally. He was the first federal Liberal leader from Queensland, the backwater state that became electoral bedrock for the Coalition and an electoral roadblock for Labor. Queensland is different. For one thing, the Liberals and Nationals are a merged entity: the Liberal National Party. The alternative prime minister and deputy prime minister – David Littleproud, the Nationals' leader – are both members of the LNP. "There is not a cigarette paper of difference between the two parties," said Dutton in 2023, regarding the federal Liberals and Nationals. In the opinion of a former LNP federal minister, Dutton is ideologically "to the right" of Littleproud.

Six of the first seven federal Liberal leaders were from Victoria. Six of the next seven first-time Liberal leaders were from Sydney. In the 1970s, the ideological heartbeat of the Liberal Party began migrating north: from Victoria, through New South Wales, and finally to the Sunshine State.

"The most toxic thing that happened to the Liberal Party brand was the Liberals and Nationals coming together as one party in Queensland," says a former Liberal federal cabinet minister from Victoria. "It was basically a National takeover of the Liberals. That was never going to fly in Melbourne."

For all the babble about inner-city elites after Howard, the Liberals continued to draw leaders from the south. Brendan Nelson was a doctor and former president of the Australian Medical Association who held a seat on Sydney's North Shore. Tony Abbott and Joe Hockey – North Shore private schoolboys – were replaced as prime minister and treasurer by Malcolm Turnbull and Scott Morrison, GPS boys from Sydney's eastern suburbs.

Dutton isn't so happy-go-lucky. He views the world with the pessimism of a Russian novelist. The son of a Brisbane bricklayer, he bombed out of university to become a copper. His earnest conservatism comes from the gut instincts of a suburban upbringing and the racial tensions of being a police officer in Queensland; not from the anti-abortion bootcamps of Bob Santamaria, nor the sermons of Brian Houston.

"I am not the evangelical here, not out and proud on abortion," Dutton told Niki Savva for her book *Plots and Prayers*. "I voted for gay marriage."

Dutton hasn't fabricated an identity based on feedback from focus groups. "ScoMo" spoke like a NIDA student's idea of a Queenslander. "Dutts," as mates call him, doesn't strain for an ocker accent or drape himself in sporting paraphernalia. His persona? A sombre straightshooter. One tough hombre. The bad cop.

Some liberals worry that gung-ho Dutton lacks the soft touch required to rebuild John Howard's broad church. He is popular with "the base." But not so much with female professionals. Liberal MP Bridget Archer, from Tasmania, feels marginalised with fewer moderates around. "When I go to Canberra and sit in the party room with Peter Dutton, Tony Pasin and Alex Antic, I think: who are these people?'

Archer claims that her views haven't changed: the party itself is shifting to the right. "The Liberal Party has become One Nation lite," she tells me.

*

On becoming leader, Dutton made it clear that he wasn't losing a great deal of sleep over the seats lost to the teals. The downsized party room wouldn't allow him much wriggle room on climate change and social issues.

"Our policies will be squarely aimed at the forgotten Australians, in the suburbs, across regional Australia," he said, adapting Robert Menzies' phrase.

This is the cultural landscape that Dutton came from. He is a Howard battler gone gangbusters: a copper turned property developer with a distrust of limp-wristed intellectuals, plus a requited lust for money. Hence he emphasises bad memories from his nine-year career as a cop, rather than happier memories from a three-decade hot streak as a property investor.

Many of Dutton's detractors underestimate the popularity of cops. In the 2021 Reader's Digest Australia Most Trusted Brands Survey, police officers were ranked sixth on the list of most trusted occupations, between scientists at fifth and schoolteachers at seventh. In contrast, journalists were twenty-ninth. Politicians – at rock bottom – were below delivery drivers, bouncers and influencers. Dutton's biggest roadblock to the public liking him isn't that he was a copper once, but that he decided to become a politician.

Those addicted to the news cycle often forget how passionately apathetic most Australian voters are about politics. As a result, Dutton's relatively small cliques of left-wing decriers and right-wing admirers overestimate how vividly the intricacies of his controversial career have registered with the general public. "I know fuck-all about him, mate," says Mark, forty-four, a loyal LNP voter. "Seems pretty boring. I miss ScoMo. He had a personality."

Mark is a tradie in outer-suburban Brisbane, with a Southern Cross tattoo and zero pity for boat people. Dutton should be right up his alley. But Mark doesn't know him from the proverbial bar of soap. Nor do most of the people you ask who don't pay all that much attention to politics. "I know of him," says Sam, twenty-nine, a Lebanese-Australian Uber driver from Western Sydney. "But I don't *know* him. He can't be worse than ScoMo, bro."

Disengaged voters occasionally see Dutton's unsmiling face on the 6 p.m. news, or hear his unpoetic monotone on radio news bulletins. They were never going to fall in love with him at first sight or soundbite. They certainly don't see him as Australia's saviour, as does shock jock Ray Hadley. But they don't hate him in the way that his foes pray. "Dutton was a cop, wasn't he?" asks Karen, sixty-nine, a Labor voter in the seat of Macquarie. "At least he had a real job. He's not a career politician."

When Dutton became the Opposition leader, lefties were elated and complacent. Australia had too many feminists; too many migrants; too many millennial renters for Dutton to win an election. Labor MPs told Albanese to go easy on Dutton, fearing that he might get knifed before they could benefit. The consensus? Dutton was unelectable. Much like John Howard, and Tony Abbott. And indeed, Albanese himself.

"The chattering classes thought that Dutton was great for Labor," says Cheryl Kernot, the former Democrats leader turned Labor MP, whom Dutton defeated for the seat of Dickson in 2001. "I think they're wrong. He reminds me of John Howard. Rat cunning. Hide of a rhino."

A Coalition unshackled from the electoral pragmatism of regaining Wentworth and Kooyong might seem easier to beat in the short term. But Dutton doesn't need to become prime minister to redraw the battlelines of Australian politics. His fight with Albanese over the suburbs and regions was always going to drag the political conversation rightwards: on race, immigration, gender and the pace of a transition away from fossil fuels. And in the seats that matter to Dutton, Labor is vulnerable to attack. "I'm not the prettiest bloke on the block," he said, after Labor's Tanya Plibersek compared his appearance to Voldemort, "but I hope I'm going to be pretty effective."

Dutton's aim is to mercilessly disturb Albanese's peacekeeping mission. To enflame the suspicion among swinging voters that Labor is more worried about delivering do-gooder platitudes than lowering their electricity bills, and more worried about social equality than the cost of living. To reframe Labor's centrist agenda as a betrayal of the Australian way of life. Dutton's raison d'être? Make Australia Afraid Again. Then he will offer himself as the lesser of two evils. A serious strongman for the age of anxiety.

*

For Peter Dutton to succeed *without* the traditional blue-ribbon Liberal seats, he would need Australia to have its own Trump moment. But he would also need that electoral rebellion against the "elites" to occur in outer-metropolitan and provincial seats, not within the rural ones already overwhelmingly held by the Coalition. "I knew what would work in marginal seats," Dutton told Niki Savva, following his botched leadership coup against Malcolm Turnbull in 2018. "I could have campaigned on law and order."

Wyatt Roy used to be the Liberal MP for the marginal Queensland seat of Longman, adjoining Dutton's outer-suburban one. Roy became – by his own admission – "Malcolm Turnbull's number-one ticket holder." Roy and Dutton differ on some things, but Roy likes him on a personal level. "I think people underestimate Peter," Roy tells me. "He is very electable. Tony Abbott was prime minister. That was in 2013, not thirty years ago. And Dutton is a much more pragmatic and formidable politician than Abbott."

Colleagues – past and present – paint a more thoughtful portrait of Dutton. To them, he is a listener, not a big noter. A gentleman, not a sleazebag. A team player, willing to do the dirty work unpalatable to moderates. He rarely loses his temper, even during heated debates. Disciplined, risk-averse and across the details. Character traits totally at odds with the public image of a chest-beating populist. "Peter has a lot of good personal qualities that other people in the recent past haven't had," Liberal senator Andrew Bragg – a moderate from Sydney – tells me. "You might not always agree on an issue. But there's no sociopathic behaviour going on."

This other Dutton is often dismissed as a Liberal PR campaign to rehabilitate a new leader with baggage. But there are many non-Liberals with nothing to gain who say it too. "Abbott was an incredibly eccentric human being," a senior Labor minister tells me. "Morrison was unhealthily self-obsessed. Dutton isn't either of those things. He is more grounded in reality."

How does the private Dutton square with the public Dutton? It doesn't, and it does. There is a method to the venom. Dutton is prepared to hurt certain groups of people to defend others. Being hated by complete strangers is the cost of winning. And beating Labor is more important than popularity. "You dirty lefties are too easy," Dutton tweeted in 2011.

Dutton's list of political hitjobs is arguably far more offensive than Abbott's. But they served a calculated purpose. Abbott just had foot in mouth disease. The Mad Monk's holy trinity – Jesus, the Queen and the ovaries of Australian women – was too idiosyncratic. Dutton's fixations – crime, race and national security – are timeless political issues. Under the right circumstances, his lack of compassion and charisma might be irrelevant. "People never spoke about John Howard's charisma," said Dutton in 2017. "At many times during John Howard's career, he was deeply unpopular."

Dutton is imitating Howard. But this is a more reactionary conservatism, with much less emphasis on economics and much less subtlety on race relations. He swapped Howard's dog whistle for a foghorn. Love him or loathe him, Howard was the master of understatement. He worried Australians in one breath and comforted them in the next.

"Peter is not remotely in the same league as John Howard," Malcolm Turnbull tells me. "Even his best friend wouldn't compare them."

There has been no ongoing attempt by Dutton to redefine himself, the way that Howard did throughout the late '80s and early '90s. Howard wanted to rearrange the way that people related to money and to the country. In the meantime, he provided support for Keating's economic reforms. Howard failed, and adjusted, and won. Through trial and error, he learnt how to package his individualistic vision as part of a patriotic narrative.

Dutton is the paperback version of Howard: the same message but less weight. Economics is not his emotional priority, beyond a tribal allegiance to tax loopholes for the rich; penalties for the poor; and hostility to trade unions. This is why he spends most of the time fighting culture wars. His grievances are well practised and sincerely held. But the moment he moves off his preferred turf, Dutton becomes clumsy and unconvincing.

"Peter is not an original thinker," says Turnbull. "I cannot recall him ever having a positive idea in the times when I was with him in government."

Dutton is the anti-ideas man. Uncreative, perhaps. But this does give him an incredible clarity as a politician. The Opposition leader is playing Whac-A-Mole against Labor. He is banking on history to keep repeating itself. And that he can smash the agents of change with the cat-like reflexes of Pat Rafter.

One moderate who doesn't underestimate Dutton is former Liberal Party attorney-general George Brandis, an old factional foe also from Queensland. He retired from politics after losing a furious power struggle with Dutton over the Home Affairs portfolio. Brandis suggests that Dutton's "slightly slow voice" and lack of intellectual flair lulled Turnbull into a false sense of security. "I think Dutton has taken a while to live down this 'he's just a copper from Queensland' image," says Brandis. "Well, he was a police officer. He is from Queensland. That doesn't make him dumb. And he isn't."

Brandis puts Dutton in a separate category to Abbott on the Liberal Party side, and to Julia Gillard and Albanese on the Labor side. He believes they would have been satisfied with being a senior government minister. The prime ministership was a nice prize, but not their sole priority.

Brandis views Dutton more in the mould of Howard, Turnbull and Kevin Rudd: politicians consumed with desire for the top job from the minute they entered parliament. "The thing about Peter … is he's very ambitious," says Brandis. "He really, really badly wants to be prime minister. He's very purposeful. Very methodical. And very strategic."

Dutton is a conundrum, then. A power-hungry strongman who isn't a clinical narcissist. A shrewd establishment politician who brazenly plays the race card. Seemingly extreme. Yet every single thing that he does is calculated to achieve his dream of becoming prime minister. It is not totally impossible he will get there one day. But who is Peter Craig Dutton? How did he get this way? And what is fuelling his ruthless pursuit of power?

FOREFATHERS

To understand Peter Dutton, one must understand Queensland, the state that created him. The modern inferiority complex of the Deep North has historical origins. It was a convict colony within a convict colony. New South Wales launched its most sick and twisted criminals into the sun, where they were joined by a throng of opportunistic squatters hustling for unclaimed land. "The colonists had come here as white men and they were going to put the black man out," said politician Boyd Dunlop Morehead – a future premier of Queensland – in 1880. "The blackfellows had to go."

Queensland inherited the Native Police from New South Wales. Systematic genocide was called "dispersal." Aboriginal troopers from other tribes were recruited to do the dirty work – shooting blacks – under the command of white officers, who were under the authority of state parliament. The corpses of men, women and children were burned to destroy evidence. "It was all very well for quasi-humanitarians, while they sat in the ease of their armchairs, to say it was a shame," said Morehead. "[They] could afford to philosophise and moralise and be very good."

Dutton's roots run deep in Queensland history. His great-great-great-grandfather was Richard James Coley. Coley became the first sergeant-at-arms of the Queensland parliament. In 1861, Captain Coley testified at a Select Committee into the Native Police. He accused the local blacks of cannibalism against their own race and homicide against whites. He also spoke openly about the reign of terror against Aboriginals pre–Native Police.

"On the Kilcoy Station, owned by Mr Evan Mackenzie, there were two white men killed, and an imported bull," said Captain Coley. "And their retaliation was very severe on the blacks – they killed hundreds of them."

"In what way?" asked the chairman.

"By shooting and poisoning them," said Coley.

"What with?" asked the chairman.

"With strychnine and arsenic, in flour," said Coley.

From then on, the local Aboriginals nicknamed strychnine "Mackenzie." Coley mentioned hearing from another farmer who claimed to have poisoned seventy blacks at a station north of Brisbane. Yet the Select Committee did little to stem the murders. Indeed, the inquiry justified the actions of the Native Police as the lesser of two evils. "Have the blacks been quieter since the establishment of a Native Police force, or not?" a member of the Select Committee asked the sergeant-at-arms.

"Much quieter," said Captain Coley.

There were no legal repercussions for the mass poisoning at Kilcoy attested to by Captain Coley. A few years later, Coley shot himself in the head with a horse pistol. He was posthumously diagnosed with temporary insanity. His son, Richard Jr, subsequently committed suicide too, with strychnine.

Richard Coley Sr's grieving daughter – Martha Ann Alice Coley – married a squatter named Charles Boydell Dutton. Charles Dutton and his brother Henry were sheep farmers on the Central Queensland station of Bauhinia Downs. They allowed Aboriginals to be co-tenants. According to fellow squatter Oscar De Satge, the Duttons were "warm protectors [of Aboriginals] from anything like cruelty and injustice."

In 1885, the *Queensland Figaro and Punch* cynically put this down to self-interest, claiming that Charles Dutton and another squatter had "developed a decided taste for aboriginals, as providing a kind of labor which, though nasty, is cheap." Later, in the 1930s, *The Queenslander* published a second-hand recollection about Bauhinia Downs:

> From my earliest years I can remember my late father telling of a little incident that happened in his younger days and that ever seemed to mesh in his memory. Riding up to the homestead of Bauhinia Downs one day the first face that peeped out at him from the windows was that of a black gin. "Mr Dutton sit down?" (meaning "Is Mr Dutton at home?") asked my father of the dark lady. His expression may be imagined when the gin queried in reply, in perfect English: "I beg your pardon, sir?" The fact of her having been brought up as a servant

> in the Dutton household from her early days had made her a stranger to pidgin English.

In 1861, the Duttons provided a safe haven for Aboriginals from the Native Police. Charles offered the Aboriginals tomahawks. With a revolver Henry defended them from potential annihilation. The Duttons were regarded as traitors to the colonial project. Charles waged a campaign of truth-telling about the Native Police via letters to *The Sydney Morning Herald*. "Before there were any complaints about the blacks in the district, the conduct of the native police was characterised by the grossest cruelty, the most oppressive and exasperating acts," wrote Charles Dutton in a letter circa 1861.

In 1883, Charles Dutton was elected to parliament for the seat of Leichardt. Liberal premier Samuel Griffiths appointed him the Minister for Lands. He purchased a two-storey house on a leafy three-acre block in Brisbane. Dutton was lampooned by the *Queensland Figaro and Punch*, who described him as "a logical lunatic" and "an out-and-out Tory in the guise of a Liberal." "In his eyes, the wealthy land-sharks of the colony form the one class to be pre-eminently worshipped." He was influential enough that a whole suburb of Brisbane – Dutton Park – was named in his honour.

His direct descendant, Peter Dutton, has been reticent about this connection to colonial Queensland. Perhaps because he isn't interested in family history. Perhaps because it doesn't mesh with his persona as a political outsider: a humble copper from nowhere and not much. To be fair, the money and social prestige didn't last. Charles Dutton's son, Henry Coley Dutton, lost a fortune in the catastrophic drought of 1902. Henry sold Bauhinia Downs and ended up running a station on the northern outskirts of Brisbane. Peter Dutton's grandfather – Henry Charles Boydell Dutton – was a linesman in Hendra, hardly part of a squatter aristocracy.

Peter Dutton's main inheritance from this era of history is political and psychological, rather than economic. The Sunshine State was presided over by a line of strongman leaders with a bipartisan propensity for populism. In Queensland, there is a rich vein of suspicion towards the south. Nowadays, this manifests as a desire for attention from federal politicians. Originally, it came from a desire to be invisible. To be left alone. The massacres happened later in the Sunshine State.

What was the body count of this multi-decade invasion? In the early 1980s, historian Henry Reynolds tentatively estimated that between 8000 and 10,000 Aboriginals were killed in Queensland. More recently, historians Raymond Evans and Robert Ørsted-Jensen estimated that at least 65,180 Aboriginals were killed on the Queensland frontier. "We are acutely sensitive to the wider denialist mood in some sectors of Australian society and its mainstream media," wrote Evans and Ørsted-Jensen in their report, "and so we proceed with caution and conservative assessment."

Reynolds was dismissed as part of a cabal of left-wing academics offering a "black armband" view of Australian history. He believes that Evans and Ørsted-Jensen have "an unrivalled knowledge of Queensland's historical records" and "have to be taken very seriously." Nonetheless, they would be regarded as certifiable lunatics by conservative critics. What can't be denied is the culture of racism that permeated the colonisation of Queensland, or the continuing unwillingness to shine a spotlight on the past.

Hence the easygoing amnesia up north. Hence the hypersensitivity to scrutiny from self-righteous outsiders. It is no coincidence that so many Queenslanders have a complicated relationship with debates about race. Better to let bygones be bygones, especially when the bygones weren't that long ago.

*

Australians were desperate to sterilise the terror of a sunburnt country. New houses sprawled outwards from the cities. Middle-class Protestants sought shelter from the soot, sewerage, sin and viral diseases of the industrial slums. Cramped terraces were traded for quarter-acre blocks. The suburbs were a blank slate, as if everyone came down in the last shower. "What may have begun as a simple forgetting of other possible views turned into habit and over time into something like a cult of forgetfulness practised on a national scale," said W.E.H. Stanner in the 1968 Boyer Lectures.

Robert Menzies stared into the heart of the Australian suburbs and found the path to a political dynasty. First, he endured a brief and unhappy stint as prime minister. Then he brooded on how to expand the electoral base of a centre-right political party in Australia. In 1942, he delivered his "Forgotten People" speech. "One of the best instincts in us is that which induces us to have one little patch of earth with a house and garden which is ours," Menzies intoned over the wireless.

This was pitched at the mass of middle-class people who didn't have the representation of the trade union movement, or the money and political access of big business. Menzies understood the Australian dream. But the suburbs he lionised were more homogenously middle-class than modern Australia. Menzies became their patrician mascot. He was unashamedly pretentious. An uncultivated heckler purportedly asked him what he was going to do about *'ousing*. "Put a *h* in front of it," quipped Menzies.

Menzies mastered the art of identity politics. He implored people to see themselves as citizens, rather than workers. And he persuaded suburbanites to turn their votes – along with their homes – into signals of virtue. Labor was too obsessed with the hip pocket nerve to nourish culture and higher education. "The middle class provides more than any other the intellectual life which marks us off from the beast; the life which finds room for literature, for the arts, for science, for medicine and the law," said Menzies – an ex-barrister – in the "Forgotten People" speech.

In the aftermath of the speech, Menzies created the Liberal Party. It was a motley crew of liberals and conservatives, glued together by a mutual opposition to Labor. Menzies supported Keynesianism, without the class hatreds and bank takeovers. There was no radical economic agenda. Simply being in power was mostly enough, because it prevented the excesses of the Left. Menzies preached "a liberal and progressive faith" to potential followers. "There is no room in Australia for a party of reaction," he said in 1944. "There is no useful place for a policy of negation."

The embryonic Liberal Party merged with the Australian Women's National League. In return for their branch members and fundraising capabilities, the AWNL secured female quotas at the upper echelons of the party. Menzies placed the fairer sex at the heart of the Liberal Party's electoral pitch. The Liberals enjoyed an advantage over Labor with women, public servants and the university-educated. In 1949, Menzies became prime minister again. The Liberal Party remained in power for the next twenty-three years. Menzies was prime minister for sixteen of them. He saw the expansion of the Australian dream as a rod to break the back of Labor. But for Menzies, there was more to life than money; more to politics than free-market economics; more to a home than capital gains. "Menzies was contemptuous of the purely materialist values and scornful of those who were driven by them," wrote Charles Kemp, the founder of the Institute of Public Affairs. "He had no great regard for businessmen."

The reincarnation of Robert Menzies would be seen as an inner-city snob by the shock jocks who serenade the modern Liberal Party. He argued – successfully, as it turned out – that Labor was too materialistic, too macho, too artless. Too consumed by hatred to appreciate the complexity of governing in the national interest. Too provincial to represent Australia with sophistication on the international stage. The lucky country should be run by centrist lawyers, not plainspoken firebrands with partisan hearts. "It would be a calamity if our applause of the age of the common man … induced us to yield to the temptation to resent or reject the uncommon man," said Menzies in 1965. "It is, after all, the uncommon man who initiates ideas."

SWINGS AND ROUNDABOUTS

Peter Craig Dutton is fervently suburban. He rose from the lower-middle-class mortgage belt north of Brisbane as if it were a seminary. His soul is beholden to a deep faith in the often paradoxical virtues of cultural stability and economic transformation. In this way, he is not dissimilar to millions of Australians. "I come from the suburbs and I have never changed my values or forgotten where I came from," said Dutton in 2022.

His dad, Bruce, was a staunchly Catholic bricklayer. His mum, Ailsa, was an Anglican secretary. They got married in a country where the old religious divisions were beginning to dissolve, eclipsed by racial ones created by the end of the White Australia policy, and the onset of debates about black land rights. The Duttons owned a nice two-storey home on Colthorpe Street in outer-suburban Boondall. It was brick – the fruit of Bruce's labours – with a tiled roof. Overhead powerlines. Blue skies, until the thunderstorms arrived. Peter – the eldest child of five – was born in 1970. There remained a hint of sectarian tension within the household. Peter gravitated more to his Anglican mother. The Duttons kept a pet parrot. "Who's a pretty boy?" it squawked.

Peter attended Boondall State Primary School. The shy, sheltered first child was wise beyond his years, and sensitive to the economic pressures on his parents. Bruce started a building business. Ailsa did the bookwork and picked up childcare work. "They didn't have much money," said Dutton. "I remember the difficult conversations around our kitchen table as we pored over the family budget trying to find ways to pay the next bills and cut back expenses."

The Duttons scrimped and saved to send Peter to a private high school: St Paul's, an all-boys Anglican college. It was fifteen minutes northwest in semi-rural Bald Hills. There were cow paddocks beyond the football fields. For families like the Duttons, a private-school education was a pathway to discipline and financial security, not intellectual self-indulgence.

Peter knew the value of a dollar. At the age of twelve, he got a job at a local butcher. It was cash-in-hand. Dutton supplemented the income with other side hustles: mowing lawns and delivering newspapers. At St Paul's, he flew under the radar. "I was not a committed student at school," he said in 2022. "I was more interested in making money."

His modest self-appraisal is corroborated by a classmate. Robin Carter attended St Paul's with Peter Dutton between 1983 and 1987. Carter – a gay man – remembers plenty of tyrants at high school, who belittled the mildest differences. Dutton wasn't one of them. But nor was he an academic. "Peter wasn't the brightest star in the sky," says Carter. "He *definitely* wasn't a nerd. But he wasn't a jock. He was pretty much invisible, to be honest." Which makes Dutton quite an outlier by the standards of high-profile politicians, who – whatever their varying political beliefs and personality traits – generally share the innate belief from an early age that they are more interesting than other people and deserve to be showered with attention and agreement.

*

It was a fertile time for Queensland conservatism. In 1974, Bob Katter was elected to the Queensland state parliament. His seat, Flinders, had been held by Labor before the split of 1955, when Bob Santamaria led an exodus of Catholics from the ALP, including Katter's father. After the split, the National Party embarked on a thirty-two-year reign over Queensland.

"Everyone outside of Brisbane was Labor," says Katter. "You were a Martian if you didn't vote for Labor! Then Labor splits in two. And half ends up in the Country Party. A bunch of hayseeds who couldn't read or write."

In Queensland, the National Party were the top dogs of the Coalition. Partly thanks to the decentralised population. Partly thanks to the parochialism of the people. And partly thanks to Labor abolishing the Legislative Council and gerrymandering the electorates of the lower house so that rural seats had an outsized power. Katter sums up Old Labor's attitude towards corruption thus: "Who gives a fuck?" "Excuse my language," he says. "Who gives a bugger about that? Righto. So they did a bit of bushranger stuff … But at the end of the day, the job got done."

This is the lingering political psychology of Queensland in a nutshell. Do whatever it takes to make the state rich, even if some corners need to be cut. Joh Bjelke-Petersen – a peanut farmer from Kingaroy who became the premier in 1968 – didn't invent the system, or the psyche behind it. But he took it to the nth degree. "There are more ways of killing a cat than drowning it," Bjelke-Petersen once remarked. "Different occasions warrant different methods of annihilating a socialist government."

Over the next nineteen years, Bjelke-Petersen showed all the different ways to drown a socialist. His reach breached the Tweed border. He helped orchestrate the dismissal of Gough Whitlam by refusing to accept Labor's nominated replacements for a Senate vacancy. He also abolished inheritance taxes, provoking the southern states to follow suit. And he hated journalists with a passion. "The greatest thing that could happen to Queensland and the nation is when we get rid of all the media," he said. "Then we could live in peace."

Bjelke-Petersen turned Queensland into a police state. The Hillbilly Dictator persecuted protestors and Aboriginal activists, while supporting apartheid in South Africa. He referred to the Labor Party as "ten little n****r boys" for their policies on Indigenous affairs. And he secretly tried to deny HIV/AIDs treatments to Aboriginal communities. "Couldn't be fairer," said Bjelke-Petersen, when asked about his treatment of Aboriginal Australians.

Bjelke-Petersen made plenty of people incredibly rich. The Gold Coast was turned from sand and mangroves into an international tourist destination. Central Queensland was transformed from a giant cattle yard into a coalmining hub. "So much for corruption," says Katter. "[Joh] never took a free cup of water! Now, I'm not saying he didn't do a lot of jobs. And those people were *very* generous to our political party."

At the 1983 election, the Nationals won forty-one of Queensland's eighty-two seats. Bjelke-Petersen recruited two Liberal MPs and secured an outright majority. It was the beginning of the end. The White Shoe Brigade – a clique of Gold Coast property developers that included Clive Palmer – hatched a psychotic plot to replace Bob Hawke with Bjelke-Petersen. The "Joh-for-PM" campaign was an attempted takeover of the federal National Party. "While the cat's away, the mice will play," says Katter.

The Joh-for-PM campaign was derailed by accusations of corruption. It still managed to kibosh Howard's first attempt to become prime minister. Howard responded to the loss of the 1987 election with a platform to wind back the fad of multiculturalism; resist a treaty with Australia's Indigenous people; and to continue as "one nation and one future." Howard also suggested that immigration from Asia should be reduced.

The leadership of the Liberal Party can be broken into three historical epochs, with some slippages in between. The Highbrow Liberals, led by Menzies. The Middlebrow Liberals, led by Howard. And eventually the Lowbrow Liberals, led by Peter Dutton. The elitism of Menzies and Fraser slowly blurred into the anti-intellectualism of Joh Bjelke-Petersen.

*

Bruce and Ailsa Dutton waited until their eldest son graduated from high school before announcing their separation. Peter – a stickler for stability – felt humiliated. He attributed the split partly to the increasing economic pressures on his parents; economic pressures that he squarely attributed to the Labor Party. "Paul Keating almost destroyed my Dad's small business with his heartless mismanagement of the economy," tweeted Dutton in 2019.

High interest rates, family breakdown and Paul Keating awakened an unforeseen zeal in Peter Dutton. At eighteen, he joined Australia's pre-eminent defender of nuclear middle-class families in the suburbs: the Liberals. His future guru, John Howard, remained leader of the party.

Dutton rose through the ranks of the Young Liberals, while studying for a business degree at the Queensland University of Technology. He was the first person in the family to receive a tertiary education. In 1989, Dutton successfully sought Liberal preselection for the state seat of Lytton, on Brisbane's southside. Lytton was held by Labor's Tom Burns on an impregnable margin of 16.3 per cent. It was a curious thing to do. The Liberals were at a low ebb, especially in Queensland. They held ten seats in state parliament: twenty less than Labor, and thirty-nine less than the Nats.

For a profile with *The Courier Mail*, a young Dutton wore a striped designer shirt. Fist on his chin to show off a leather watch. Suntanned and handsome, with a thick, wavy fringe. His political priority at eighteen? Homelessness. He released no philosophical manifesto. But at this stage, the young man from the suburbs evoked Menzies more than Bjelke-Petersen. "A lot of the older politicians perhaps are stuck in their way," said Dutton in a TV interview with the ABC, wearing a debonair suit and tie. "Young blood has to come through and hopefully this will start the ball rolling."

Initially, Dutton wasn't rewarded for going against the grain. Post-Joh, the Nationals lost in a landslide. Under the leadership of Wayne Goss, Labor secured government for the first time since 1957. Dutton was smashed at the ballot box: Burns received a 6.2 per cent swing. "It was a big mistake to run an eighteen-year-old in a seat where 50 per cent of the people are over fifty," said a commentator on the ABC's election coverage.

"Boy wonder indeed," said host Andrew Olle.

Adding insult to injury, Dutton failed four out of six subjects in his first year at QUT: computing for accounting, managerial accounting, business finance, and introduction to law. Robert Menzies he was not. After just one year, he scaled back to part-time studies. And over the next decade, he continued to fail university subjects. Dutton is one of the few recent would-be prime ministers who can empathise with academic underachievers. "I didn't enjoy accounting whatsoever," he said.

Some important lessons had been learnt. In Queensland, the Liberals' main threat came from its right flank. Up north, the Liberal Party needed to cultivate a pineapple-flavoured conservatism to flourish – somewhere between Howard and Bjelke-Petersen. And to reclaim the lost power of the Dutton family, Peter would need to bypass the knowledge class.

In 1989, the Fitzgerald Inquiry uncovered widespread bribes made to Queensland cops. The police force had operated a protection racket for illegal gambling and prostitution. A former police commissioner, Terry Lewis, was charged with corruption, perjury and forgery. He ended up spending ten and a half years in prison. "I was sort of fascinated by that period," said Dutton.

After dropping out of university, the contrarian teenager became chair of the Bayside Young Liberals. And he joined a public institution even more beleaguered in Queensland than the Coalition: the police force. It offered rigid discipline, group identity and a good wage. It also provided Dutton a shortcut to power, the desire that had proved unfulfilled at the state election.

The Queensland police force welcomed cleanskins with open arms. The old-school cops who had survived the Fitzgerald Inquiry didn't. They smelt rats in the ranks. Constable Dutton addressed the doubts of his sceptical elders by going for the jugular of petty criminals. A former colleague – Stephen Angus – recalled Dutton's relish for playing the "bad cop" role. "He is strongly conservative in his old-world values," Angus told *QWeekend*. "He is very, very loyal … It is like [Dutton] was born in the 1950s."

While most politicians of his generation were cosplaying as JFK and Margaret Thatcher at sandstone university campuses, Dutton was studying Australia's underbelly. He confronted drug addiction and suicides. As a young constable, Dutton was sent north to toughen him up. He was stationed in Townsville, an army town with a large black population. Violence defined his first impressions of Aboriginal culture. "[I] still live with those images of turning up to domestic violence incidences where Indigenous women and children had suffered physical abuse," said Dutton in 2023.

Palm Island was a 23-minute plane ride away. It had been established as a convict camp for recalcitrant Aboriginals. Now their descendants were technically free, but mostly imprisoned by abject poverty. "I remember clearly attending Palm Island where I brought back the body of an Indigenous woman in a body bag who had been thrust off a cliff to her death," said

Dutton in 2023. He cited these experiences as a key reason for boycotting Kevin Rudd's apology to the Stolen Generations in 2008.

The Fitzgerald Inquiry wasn't the only source of bitterness for Queensland cops of that era. In 1987, the Hawke government launched a Royal Commission into Aboriginal Deaths in Custody. No police officer had been charged for the death of an Indigenous person under their care. The report was published in 1991. It made 339 recommendations, including that Aboriginal and Torres Strait Islander people should only be arrested as a last resort, and not for profanity. Also, that politicians should provide bipartisan support for reconciliation to avoid "division, discord, and injustice." Paul Keating took heed. "The report of the Royal Commission into Aboriginal Deaths in Custody showed with devastating clarity that the past lives on in inequality, racism and injustice," said Keating in the Redfern speech.

Less than a decade earlier, the ALP had been led by Bill Hayden, an ex-cop from Queensland. Race deepened the fissure between the Labor Party and its working-class base, especially police officers. Dutton was intensely loyal to a public institution – the police force – that had been operating with impunity. Keating broke the nation's bro code. He shone a spotlight on the violence and lies hiding inside the Great Australian Silence.

*

In his spare time, Peter Dutton joined the family business: Dutton Holdings. He and his father bought and sold properties across Queensland. At twenty, Peter had acquired his first home: a $93,000 unit in Yeronga, next door to Dutton Park. He sold it two years later for $116,500. His second investment was a house in Murrumba Downs. He bought it with his father for $60,000.

At the age of twenty-two, Dutton got married. He expected to have kids and live "happily ever after," unlike his parents. But it wasn't just at work where legal loopholes were making mincemeat of moral absolutes. His first marriage lasted five months. "And, yeah, so we just came home one day," Dutton said in 2023. "Not in love anymore. And that was the end of it."

Dutton's Australian dream was in tatters. At this stage, he was a divorcee consumed by a desire for order yet taught by experience that failure, pain and sin reign supreme. Proof of this imbalance kept accumulating.

Sonny Paul Graham was a Māori man born in Auckland. He began committing burglaries at the age of fifteen. At the age of twenty-one, he emigrated to Australia. In Queensland, he served a twelve-month prison sentence for breaking and entering, assault causing bodily harm, and vandalism. Graham was released from prison, but he wasn't deported to New Zealand. Throughout 1994, Graham prowled Brisbane, attempting break-ins and looking out for women to rape.

On 22 October, at about 5 a.m., a drunken Graham failed to break into a series of units occupied by women. At 5:30 a.m., Graham found a house with an unlocked front door. The 27-year-old snuck inside. A ten-year-old girl was asleep in bed. Her dad was asleep on the couch in the lounge room. Her mum metres away in the bathroom. Graham woke the girl up. He told her to keep quiet. Then he tried to rape her, both vaginally and anally. She resisted. He punched her in the face and kept going.

This was recounted in a 2014 *Good Weekend* profile of Peter Dutton by Madonna King titled 'Good Cop, Bad Cop'. Dutton, twenty-three, was a detective on the case. He was gripped by a soul-altering level of adrenaline and moral disgust. "I can remember going to crime scenes where a young girl had been raped," said Dutton in 2023. "To this day, you can still remember the full name of the victim; the offender; the dates of birth; the times. And still picture that scene."

With a composite sketch, Dutton hunted through the area eliminating suspects. Graham was arrested. He pleaded guilty. The judge sentenced him to twelve and a half years in prison. Parole would be available after five years. Dutton was revolted by the discrepancy between the crime and the punishment. The victim suffered from serious psychiatric issues. Her trauma was a life sentence. "The sexual assault of children is something I cannot comprehend," said Dutton in 2014. "It upsets me greatly."

Dutton's lust for justice was thwarted by the legal system. He found a fresh set of enemies: the cosmopolitan knowledge class, who prioritised abstract ideals learnt at university over the common-sense desires of the mob. "He is not a big fan of lawyers, Peter Dutton," George Brandis – an Oxford-educated barrister – tells me. "I've never met a policeman who was, to be honest … I can understand how police would arrest somebody; have no doubt that they were guilty; and then see them acquitted because of the skill of their barrister."

Raymond John Carroll was the main suspect in the unsolved murder of Deidre Kennedy. Deidre was a blonde toddler. In 1973, she was abducted from her cot. Just seventeen months old. Her body was found on the roof of a toilet block in Limestone Park, Ipswich. Dressed in a pair of women's underwear. Human bite marks on the legs. She had been sexually assaulted and strangled to death. In 1983, Raymond Carroll was arrested for stealing and defacing lingerie and photos belonging to women. The fetishised nature of the crime attracted interest from Deidre's investigators. Carroll's unique overbite matched the bite marks on her legs. He was charged. Everyone in Queensland wanted his scalp. The jury convicted him of murder.

The decision was overturned by the court of appeal, due to insufficient evidence. Throughout the 1990s, police found new evidence linking Carroll to the crime. Dutton staged surveillance on him. But Carroll couldn't be charged a second time, owing to double jeopardy laws. "Peter has really been my rock," said Faye Kennedy – Deidre's mother – in 2007. "He was a police officer and actually worked on bubby's case."

Shortly before Dutton quit the Queensland Police Force, Carroll was charged with perjury for lying in his murder trial. It was an innovative legal manoeuvre. Later, a jury found Carroll guilty. He appealed. The High Court upheld the ruling of double jeopardy. Carroll was back on the streets.

These painful experiences explain the irrevocable moral high ground that Dutton occupies. Civilisation isn't just a diplomatic fracas about capital. It is a black-and-white battle between good and evil. Dutton was on the side of saints. This worldview might have made him a great detective. It made him an undeniable source of emotional support for the victims of crime. But it also blinded him to the shades of grey in everyday events.

*

A backlash had been brewing against the fashionable compassion of politicians and judges, especially in Queensland. Someone needed to speak the truth about crime, race and the perils of porous borders. Enter Pauline Hanson. The flame-haired single mum owned a fish and chip shop in Ipswich, west of Brisbane. She gained Liberal Party preselection for the seat of Oxley. At the start of 1996, Hanson watched with disgust as Robert Tickner – Keating's Indigenous Affairs minister – preached the need for the justice system to show more leniency. Hanson sent a letter to *The Queensland Times*.

"Black deaths in custody seem to be Robert Tickner's latest outcry," she wrote. "Pity that as much media coverage or political grandstanding is not shown for white deaths in custody. As for Tickner's statement that Aborigines should not go to jail because apparently it is not working: imagine what type of country this would be to live if Aborigines didn't go to jail for their crimes."

Hanson's missive is better remembered for her comment about people receiving welfare despite having a "minute" amount of Aboriginal blood. But crime was one of her fundamental obsessions. This enamoured her to many Old Labor voters. Plenty of working-class people were nostalgic for the death penalty. They found the liberalism of cosmopolitans incomprehensible.

Alas, Hanson hadn't learnt how to muffle her attacks on Aboriginal people into dog whistles. The Liberals dumped her as a candidate. Hanson ran as a rogue independent and sensationally flipped a safe Labor seat. In her maiden speech, she criticised the reverse racism of the politically correct elite. "In response to my call for equality for all Australians, the most noisy criticism came from the fat cats, bureaucrats and the do-gooders," she said.

Howard won the 1996 election with a majority of blue-collar voters. The new prime minister refused to rebuke Hanson. He tried to seduce her followers to the Liberal Party. Peter Dutton sympathised with Hanson's views on law and order. "One of Hanson's attractions to the broader public was her former 'tough on criminals' approach," wrote Dutton in 2003. "Much of the criticism came from the usual suspects among the academic and media elite."

Jeannine Smith was the mother of three young children. She was also a self-confessed regular marijuana smoker. In 1996, she was handed a suspended six-month prison sentence for giving a joint to a friend. The following year, she was arrested again for the possession of a dangerous drug and a smoking utensil. A report was submitted to the court by the Aboriginal & Torres Strait Islands Corporation. It testified to Smith's difficult background; diligent attempts at education to provide for her children; and attempts at rehabilitation. Nonetheless, the magistrate activated the suspended sentence. Smith went to prison.

In 1998, she appealed the decision in the District Court. "Peter Craig Dutton" was the respondent for the police. He was a Detective Senior Constable in the Covert Surveillance Unit. The judge concluded that "the enforcement of the full six months period was unjust." Smith was released.

That August, Dutton sat parked in an unmarked Mazda outside a fast-food restaurant in Goodna, southwest of Brisbane. He was staging surveillance on Bradley John Bell. Bell was a survivor of sexual abuse at the Sir Leslie Wilson Youth Detention Centre in Brisbane. He used heroin and meth to self-medicate severe PTSD. Bell left the car park in a Holden Commodore. Dutton pursued. Bell sped away, and refused to stop. Suddenly, he turned onto an unpaved road. Then he made another swift turn into a car park. Close behind him, Dutton's Mazda scraped a concrete garden bed. His vehicle flipped onto its side and slid into a building.

Dutton was knocked unconscious. Blood gushed from behind his ear. The tough cop spent three weeks convalescing from headaches and back pains. In 2000, he sued Bell's insurance company for $250,000, plus interest. "The plaintiff resigned from the Queensland police force on 30 July 1999 due to the fact that his confidence in driving was low," noted the court file.

The crash ended Dutton's police career. In 2001, Bell celebrated his fresh release from prison by breaking into the Coorparoo Police Station. He cut a 150-kg safe out of the floor. It contained sixteen Glock pistols and two Ruger revolvers. Bell hired a container to stockpile the guns, accompanying the DVD players and chainsaws that had been paid for with a stolen chequebook. In 2005, Dutton discontinued the claim against Bell's insurer. His circumstances had changed. He was now a tough-on-crime politician.

Dutton is tight-lipped and sleepy-eyed. But not because he isn't thinking or feeling anything. He is just trying to keep a lid on the din within. In 2023, an unusually vulnerable Dutton admitted to Annabel Crabb that he probably suffers from a form of undiagnosed post-traumatic stress disorder "People would refer to it, I s'pose, more frequently now as a sort of PTSD, or just the mental hangover of seeing that repeatedly," said Dutton. And then: "The attitude in those days would've been just, you know, harden up."

Dutton became a man frozen within a period of fear. Trauma made him soft. In lieu of psychological attention, control made him feel solid and safe again. Always displaying simplicity and strength. Because he feels so complicated and weak.

*

The times suited Dutton, on several fronts. He finished his business degree and went full-time into property development with his father. In 1999, John Howard introduced a 50 per cent discount on capital gains, sparking a real-estate boom.

The Duttons had bought buildings in Acacia Ridge, Logan and Bald Hills. They renovated them into childcare centres. Some were leased to companies for plum sums. Some they ran themselves. Pretty soon, they were employing forty people. Dutton's Australian dream was back on the rails.

In February 2000, a government adviser named Gracelyn Smallwood – "Australia's leading Aboriginal health expert" – was arrested in Townsville. Smallwood was doing her usual Friday-night run to provide lifts to drinkers at the Sovereign Hotel. A fight broke out. Six police cars arrived. Smallwood saw a young Aboriginal man who wasn't involved in the brawl get roughly arrested. According to the police, Smallwood accused them of acting like the Ku Klux Klan. The police arrested Smallwood and threw her into a van. She suffered spinal injuries. At the watchhouse, she was strip-searched for weapons and held for three and a half hours without legal aid.

"It is all right for police to throw Murri people into these cages and cart them off for the most undignified and belittling treatment," Smallwood told journalist Tony Koch. "It is a disgrace what is happening to my people."

Smallwood made an official complaint. Queensland Council for Civil Liberties vice-president Terry O'Gorman said the strip-searching of a woman for a public order offence was "utterly unacceptable." In a letter to *The Courier Mail*, Peter Dutton hit back. It was his first foray into public debate. "O'Gorman would be the first to complain if people in police custody were to harm themselves or another prisoner with a weapon or drugs concealed on their body," wrote Dutton. "The police have a duty of care to those in their custody and appear to be damned if they do and damned if they don't."

Dutton missed being feared and loathed by a loud minority of society on behalf of a quiet, law-abiding majority in the suburbs. That year he became secretary of the Liberal Party's Brisbane branch. Politics would enable Dutton to play the role of the bad cop without the risk of physical injury.

Peter Dutton had changed dramatically since 1989. But so had Australian politics and the Liberal Party. Howard was trying to create a broader church – externally, but also internally. He wanted to send a message to voters flirting with One Nation that the Liberals were listening.

"There were people – of whom I was one – who did regard university education as being somewhat under attack by a more populist cultural attitude," says George Brandis, who entered the federal Senate for the Liberal Party in 2000.

Dutton was an ideal candidate for Howard's new Liberal Party. It was as if Dutton had been created in an underground laboratory at Crosby Textor to embody the zeitgeist of economically aspirational and socially conservative suburbanites. "I felt that particularly … our party was dominated by lawyers, and police officers were sort of frowned upon," said Dutton.

The seat of Dickson sat on the northern fringes of Brisbane. Suburban sprawl country, with a smattering of semi-rural polling booths. Not too rich and not too poor. Ethnically, Dickson was a throwback to the country of Dutton's childhood. At the 2001 census, 81.6 per cent of the electorate was born in Australia. The next highest countries of birth were England, New Zealand, Scotland, South Africa and the Netherlands. When Cheryl Kernot defected from the Democrats to Labor, Kim Beazley parachuted his prized recruit into the Liberal-held marginal seat. In 1998, Labor lost the election but Kernot won Dickson on a margin of 0.12 per cent.

At the start of 2001, Dutton secured Liberal preselection for Dickson with the support of conservative powerbroker Santo Santoro. He didn't live there. He owned a home in Mount Cotton, on Brisbane's deep southside. "Nobody on my team knew him," says Kernot. "He hadn't been around."

That was about to change. Dutton ditched his suit and tie for ill-fitting dress shirts with open necks and short sleeves. The thirty-year-old candidate hit the hustings with gusto. Kernot was delivering a press conference outside Australia Post, protesting against the Howard government's closure of branches. A van screamed into the car park. The doors slid open. Dutton jumped out. He began heckling Kernot. They had never met. "That's him, you see," says Kernot. "He's a winner. Whatever nastiness you need to inflict along the way, that's okay. Because victory will be worth it."

Kernot's other most vivid impression of Dutton was from the Pine Rivers Show. She set up a stall in the pavilion shed as a way to talk with local constituents. From the corner of her eye, she saw Dutton leaning against a wheelie bin. For roughly twenty minutes, he ran surveillance on his opponent. As if Kernot were selling heroin – not social democracy – to elderly show-goers. "It was a little bit of intimidation," says Kernot. "He had no shame."

Underneath the façade, Dutton was suffering from plenty of shame. At election events, he apologised profusely for the non-attendance of his partner. Unbeknown to Kernot, Dutton was going to become a father. But his relationship with a woman named Rachel ended before the forthcoming birth of their daughter, Rebecca. "That was a difficult period," he said. "You describe it as a mistake at the time, but the best mistake I ever made."

Dutton met his second wife, Kirilly, on the campaign trail. She was a personal assistant to Sarina Russo, the Brisbane private employment tsar. In 2001, no divorced politician had been elected prime minister. Australians still wanted their leaders to come from nuclear families, even if their own were splintering. Dutton was a divorcee about to have a child out of wedlock.

On that first campaign, Dutton seesawed between shyness and incivility. His desire for privacy was challenged by a hunger for public conflict. He was a social conservative who craved stability, while bristling with all the moral chaos of the modern age.

*

In late August 2001, a wooden boat carrying 433 Middle Eastern asylum seekers – including forty-three children – became stranded in international waters to the north of Australia. It was sinking. The refugees were rescued by a Norwegian freighter, MV *Tampa*. There were four pregnant women on board, one suffering from abdominal pains. A group of refugees begged the captain, Arne Rinnan, to sail to Australia. He obliged. The Howard government threatened to prosecute Rinnan as a people smuggler if he continued to Christmas Island. Rinnan ignored the legal threats. So heavily armed SAS troops seized control of the Norwegian vessel. "That boat will never land in our waters – never!" John Howard declared.

Howard followed up with the Pacific Solution. Detention centres were set up on Manus Island and Nauru. Howard received an enormous boost in the polls. Less than a fortnight later, Australians woke up to the news that Al-Qaeda had flown two planes into the Twin Towers. The West was at war. Osama bin Laden was astute enough not to send plane hijackers to Australia on fishing boats. But Coalition cabinet minister Peter Reith directly linked the threat of terrorism to the arrival of undocumented asylum seekers. Suddenly, many Australians saw refugees as not just queue-jumpers or dole-bludgers but potential jihadists. And nowhere did that sentiment ring truer than in Queensland, a state with a perpetual fear of Asian invasion.

The 2001 election was a fateful moment for an ex-copper with authoritarian tendencies to embark on a political career. Dutton saw threat everywhere. Now sheltered suburbanites felt that same sense of existential panic. Dutton called for boat people to be sent packing "at the first available opportunity." He accused pro-refugee activists of being "a ratbag front for the Labor Party." The letterboxes of Dickson were flooded with patriotic pamphlets. "Labor is soft on illegal immigrants," wrote Dutton.

The Liberal Party was strong. On 7 October, HMAS *Adelaide* intercepted a sinking ship north of Christmas Island. It was carrying 219 asylum seekers, mainly Iraqis, including fifty-six children. Under strict orders, the navy towed the sinking boat towards nowhere. Eventually, it sank. Refugees leapt into the sea. The navy saved them. Photos of the rescue were used as "proof" that children had been thrown overboard by the asylum seekers so that the navy would be forced to rescue them. "The fact is that children were thrown into the water," said Defence Minister Peter Reith, a lie reiterated by Prime Minister John Howard.

Shortly afterwards, writs for the election were submitted. Kernot was on a hiding to nothing. Simultaneously, Tony Abbott – Howard's chief parliamentary headkicker – was waging war on Kernot for being a fake suburbanite. She was attacked for listing a unit on the Gold Coast as her principal place of residence. Kernot lashed out at Dutton. She accused him of "couch-surfing at a mate's place" for the campaign. "I want you to ask him why he left the police force," Kernot said to News Corp journalist Michael McKenna. "He was last in the drug squad, I understand."

Kernot was accused of "dirty tricks" and "mudslinging." Dutton called the insinuations of shady behaviour "offensive and preposterous." But he didn't clarify the exact nature of his departure at the time, and he hasn't since, despite ongoing innuendo. Perhaps because he would have felt emasculated by the truth. Dutton did produce a glowing reference from the National Crime Commission. "He wouldn't know how to be bent," said a detective.

Peter Costello called Kernot a "disgrace." Howard called for Labor to reprimand her. Kernot expressed regret for the offence caused. That night, she appeared on *Lateline* for a debate with Abbott. But she went off-script. She castigated Abbott for engineering a "three-year campaign of smear and innuendo against me and my family," now assisted by Dutton. "This is just the product of an overheated imagination," said Abbott.

*

On 10 November 2001, Howard was re-elected. The centre had shifted decisively to the right, led by Howard, and mostly followed by the shellshocked ALP. Howard had slain Malcolm Fraser and remade the Liberal Party in his own image. "'Boat vote' sinks ALP," read a headline in the *Sunday Mail*. The article claimed that the Coalition had soaked up roughly 80 per cent of the shrunken One Nation vote in Queensland. Dutton won Dickson with a primary vote swing of 10.97 per cent.

The rookie MP took off on a solemn pilgrimage to Ground Zero in New York City. He described this visit as "a chilling reminder of the reality of our short existence." On 13 February 2002, back in Australia, Dutton delivered the most incendiary maiden speech since Pauline Hanson's. His gangly body couldn't fill out the loose suit. His boyish face was playing catch-up with a deep monotone that belonged to someone decades older. "I have seen the sickening behaviour displayed by people who, frankly, barely justify their existence in our sometimes over-tolerant society," he said.

Minorities were unmentioned. Dutton had learnt from Hanson's mistakes. If he didn't mention ethnicity when talking about crime and welfare, then he was off to the races. Hanson spoke the quiet part out loud, so that those who followed could rise without the same shock to the system. "Political correctness" provided Dutton with a two-word catch-all for the agenda of intellectuals and Aboriginal activists. He directed particular ire at Terry O'Gorman's anti-Joh Civil Liberties Council:

> The fight for a better place in which to live is today made even more difficult for many reasons, not least of which is the fact that the boisterous minority and the politically correct seem to have a disproportionate say in public debate today. The Silent Majority, the Forgotten People – or the aspirational voter of our generation, as some like to term them – are fed up with bodies like the Civil Liberties Council and the Refugee Action Collective, and certainly the dictatorship of the trade union movement. Australians are fed up with the Civil Liberties Council – otherwise known as the criminal lawyers media operative – who appear obsessed with the rights of criminals yet do not utter a word of understanding or compassion for the victims of crime. Their motives are questionable and their hypocrisy breathtaking … There is a right for all people to be heard. The mood of the Silent Majority is fast rising to one of anger.

Peter Dutton was a thinking man's Pauline Hanson. "Australians generally, and Hanson supporters in particular, like strong leaders," wrote Dutton in 2003, while also pointing out that the One Nation founder had "simplistic economic policies." This was the blueprint of the New Liberals: the cultural parochialism of One Nation without the economic protectionism.

*

Dutton hit the ground running. He was afforded an astonishingly high profile for a first-term backbencher. In 2003, Dutton delivered a parliamentary speech supporting the Howard government's migration bill. It included a crackdown on identity fraud by potential terrorists.

"Once a copper, always a copper," shouted Nicola Roxon.

"What have you got against police in this country?" asked Dutton. "What are you trying to say? I do not understand."

Order was called. Dutton bollocked the ALP for not caring about terrorism or understanding the psyche of Australians. He cited the September 11 plane hijackings as justification for collecting more personal ID from migrants. This was followed by a response from Michael Hatton MP, an ex-staffer to Paul Keating. "For the edification of the Member for Dickson, the comment *once a copper, always a copper* relates to the narrow ... blinkered, black-and-white way he perceives the divide between the government and the Opposition," said Hatton.

The mockery of Dutton's old occupation set the tone for the next two decades. He was framed mostly in his preferred way: as a humble Queensland copper, not a wealthy property developer. In 2002, Dutton's family had sold three childcare centres to ABC Learning for roughly $3 million. In 2003, Dutton married Kirilly in Italy. They purchased a six-bedroom house with a swimming pool for $710,000. It was on two hectares in Camp Mountain, on the southwestern fringes of Dickson. Rebecca was followed by two sons: Harry and Tommy. At parks, their hypervigilant father didn't let them stray from his sight. "Because [I've] seen some horrific cases where children have been abducted and assaulted," he said. "It always weighs on your mind."

Dutton fiercely guarded his private life. But he was an autobiographical politician. Most start this way and are forced to compromise with the median experience. The opposite happened to Peter Dutton. His approach to public policy was guided by personal emotions. He attacked the abstract and aggregated in favour of a first-person version of the world.

Dutton joined Howard's Families and Communities Affairs Committee. It conducted an inquiry into family law and the Child Support Agency. The committee recommended increasing the rights of fathers. Dutton's previous experiences as a single father filtered his perceptions of family breakdown. "For parents to use children as pawns or to seek revenge – no matter what the circumstances – is a vile act," wrote Dutton in 2003. "When parents fall out of love with each other, they don't fall out of love with their children." Dutton wanted to remove expensive lawyers from the custody process. The Chief Justice of the Family Court, Alistair Nicholson, called the changes "unconstitutional, impractical and naive." "There is not one lawyer on that committee," said Nicholson.

Belittlement by big heads simply whetted Dutton's appetite for battle. Around this time, he panned Justice Michael Kirby for opposing the death penalty for the Bali bombers. And he supported legislation allowing businesses to refuse service to drug addicts, on the basis that they weren't suffering from a legitimate disability. Dutton also called for welfare payments to be linked to mandatory parenting courses. This would break the "cycle of hopelessness" that allowed kids to roam the streets at night. Dutton relished the backlash. "[The Silent Majority] are fed up with being pushed in a particular direction by some of the do-gooders or the ABC latte set," he said, echoing Pauline Hanson.

Dutton continued to pursue changes to Queensland's double-jeopardy laws, so that criminals like Raymond Carroll could be tried again for serious crimes. With the mother of Deirdre Kennedy, Faye, he launched a petition. It called for "Deidre's Law." The petition gained 33,000 signatures in a matter of weeks. Dutton accompanied Kennedy on a public relations campaign through Queensland. "It was nerve-racking for me," Faye Kennedy told *Good Weekend* in 2014. "I was out of my comfort zone and he just looked after me so well. His moods never changed and I believed everything he told me. I trusted him." Dutton held a press conference with Kennedy. She was too distressed to speak. He accused the state Labor government of "playing games" and sitting on its hands. Dutton was indefatigable. Eventually, the laws were changed.

At the 2004 election, Howard was re-elected for a fourth time, with a majority in the senate. In Dickson, One Nation was M.I.A. Dutton received a 6.55 per cent primary vote swing. Malcolm Turnbull entered the lower house in Wentworth. He was the ultimate insider. Dutton self-identified as an outsider. "I am not a career politician, or a barrister," read Dutton's website. "I want to bring some common sense and real life experience to the position."

What was the definition of a career politician, if not a Young Liberal who first ran for parliament at the age of nineteen, before getting elected by the age of thirty? It didn't matter. Howard promoted 33-year-old Dutton to the outer ministry. His official position was Minister for Workplace Participation. The media framed him as a straightshooter: ambitious and belligerent, but great theatre. He was Tony Abbott without the Rhodes Scholarship and peculiar theological preoccupations. Although he did vote in favour of Abbott retaining a veto on the sale of the abortion drug RU486.

Occasionally, Dutton's emulation of Abbott highlighted a spiteful side. During a debate about workforce participation, Dutton was asked a question by Michael Keenan, the new MP for Stirling. The previous MP – Labor's Jann McFarlane – was then undergoing treatment for bowel cancer. "It's great to have a live member in Stirling," quipped Dutton. Kim Beazley called it an "extraordinary slur." Dutton apologised. He was making a name for himself as someone prepared to say the unutterable. Faye Kennedy got the Dr Jekyll side of Dutton. Jann McFarlane saw his Mr Hyde side. He had a limitless capacity for kindness towards victims of particular crimes, and a parallel capacity for viciousness towards his political enemies.

A Senate majority gave the Liberal Party carte blanche to wage war against the poor. Dutton became Howard's main foot soldier. He claimed that one in five welfare recipients were dole cheats, based upon anecdotal feedback from privatised job providers. "My message to those people is you have a wake-up call coming," said Dutton. "For those people doing the wrong thing, we will come down hard."

Dutton was unflustered by structural suffering. It was to this tough nut that Howard entrusted the work-for-the-dole program. Dutton said that jobless surfers in Byron Bay should get off their boards and help drought-stricken farmers. Filmmaking and radio projects would no longer count as work. "I don't care much for programs promoting basket-weavers in Balmain," said Dutton, appropriating a phrase of Paul Keating's.

The actual victims of his policies were heavily represented in suburban and regional areas. New recipients of the disability support pension – who could work at least fifteen hours a week – would receive a $77 cut in their fortnightly allowance. Once their children reached school age, new recipients of the single parenting payment would receive a $44 cut to their fortnightly allowance. Both would be unable to collect a $31.20 weekly education supplement for TAFE and university. According to Dutton, this would incentivise them to get real jobs.

During a debate on *Lateline*, Penny Wong pointed out that most single parents affected by the payment changes were women without Year 12 certificates. What jobs would be readily available for them, especially if it would now be harder to study? In response, Dutton drew possibly the longest bow of his career-long campaign to paint Labor as the party of the elites. "The Labor Party should stop talking down to people just because they don't have a university education," he said, advocate of the Aussie battler.

In Dutton's mind, there was a thin line between welfare fraud and the drug-trafficking syndicates funding global terrorism. To kill two birds with one stone, he argued in favour of creating a national ID card. This became his trademark. He conflated seemingly unrelated issues with a straight face. So that Labor couldn't defend welfare recipients without defending terrorists. The ID card proposal provoked opposition from the Nationals' Ron Boswell and the Liberals' Bronwyn Bishop. Neither was a notable bleeding heart. George Brandis was also critical. Dutton was unchastened. He pushed on with peddling cuts to the disability and single parent payments. In Brisbane, Dutton replaced John Howard as a speaker at the Australian Council of Social Service conference. His speech drew "angry muttering and jeers." A wheelchair-bound woman departed in disgust.

"Bullshit," she muttered. Dutton left without taking questions.

*

At the start of 2006, Dutton was promoted to assistant treasurer under Peter Costello. He was a strident proponent of WorkChoices, Howard's sweeping changes in favour of employers. *The Courier Mail* revealed that the "Liberal wonderboy" responsible for a government program called "Understanding Money" had failed a string of accounting subjects at university. "Anyone who has listened to this bloke in parliament or on the radio knows he's not the sharpest tool in the shed," a Labor figure told *The Courier Mail*. "Malcolm Turnbull would be filthy he's back in the line behind this guy."

Such scoffers believed they were better judges of capability than John Howard, one of the canniest politicians in Australian history. Dutton was quarrelsome. His lexicon was fairly simple. But he wasn't a dribbling idiot. One doesn't win a marginal seat by the age of thirty and become a government minister by the age of thirty-three – sans any nepotistic connections within the media or the Liberal Party – without possessing an impressive political skillset. "Dutton is very intelligent," says George Brandis. "He is somebody who is very good at getting across a brief … Though he is not somebody who would necessarily be reading books about political philosophy."

Wedge politics required a thick hide, not an encyclopaedic knowledge of Edmund Burke. Howard handed Dutton wedges to deploy more regularly than a caddie for Greg Norman. Whatever self-doubt Dutton may have felt vanished in the fatherly gaze of the prime minister. And their spiritual connection wasn't just one-way. "When Dutton speaks, Howard listens very closely," wrote Matt Price in *The Australian*. "You can tell the PM is mentally summing up the young bloke, thinking: 'We might have a good 'un here.'"

Dutton was criticised for a conflict of interest. His family continued to receive about $100,000 a year in rent from ABC Learning for one of their remaining childcare centres. ABC Learning had just turned an $88-million profit while receiving substantial childcare rebates paid by taxpayers. ABC Learning's founder, Eddy Groves, donated $135,000 to the Coalition between 2002 and 2007. Dutton received $15,000 directly. Groves described Dutton as a "good bloke." Dutton described Groves as a "close friend." Now, as assistant treasurer, Dutton had responsibility for the childcare rebate. "ABC has a strong model providing affordable childcare," said Dutton in 2006, "and [I] am pleased to be associated with Eddie Groves and ABC."

Dutton's embrace of free-market capitalism was hot-and-cold. Big government for business. Small government for the poor. Except when the poor needed to be taught how to raise their own children. At the same time, he opposed the "nanny-state" utopia sought by bleeding-heart lefties. "Do I need Peter Garrett telling me how to raise my children?" asked Dutton in 2008. "I thought he had lots to do with whales and the environment."

Dutton had nothing against a nanny state, provided he was the one running it. He wasn't opposed to massive rebates for childcare centres. But he did want less funding allocated to welfare for disabled people, single mums and the unemployed. This would require more state paternalism, with expensive surveillance of welfare recipients and harsher punishments. Dole bludgers were "trying to rip the guts out of the system," unlike his donors.

In 2008, ABC Learning went into receivership. Groves owed over $1 billion to creditors. Dutton wasn't one of them. The rent on the church in Bald Hills that the Duttons had renovated into a childcare centre was "up to date."

Kevin Rudd was an ideas man. In the end, it took a Mandarin-speaking technocrat from Queensland to put John Howard out to pasture. WorkChoices became the millstone around Howard's neck. The prime minister lost his own seat of Bennelong. Peter Dutton won Dickson by 0.13 per cent, but suffered a swing of 8.76 per cent. "People at the moment are looking at Kevin Rudd like they're looking at a promo for *Big Brother*," said Dutton. "When the big night comes … they realise that the show is a load of crap."

Wayne Swan dismissed Dutton as a "junior woodchuck." But how much wood could a woodchuck chuck if a woodchuck could chuck wood? Rudd had won the election promising an apology to the Stolen Generations. Dutton was the new shadow finance minister. He warned that the government was opening the floodgates to a $10-billion compensation bill: "It would beggar belief that they would be contemplating an apology that could open the government up to serious damages claims."

The Liberal Party resolved to support the symbolic expression of regret. Dutton felt so strongly about not saying sorry that he tendered his resignation to Brendan Nelson. On 13 February 2008, Dutton was a no-show at the Apology, the only member of the shadow frontbench to abstain. "I regarded it as something which was not going to deliver tangible outcomes to kids who are being raped and tortured in communities," he said in 2010.

Dutton wanted to remain in a state of perpetual forgetfulness: that Great Australian Silence. Which was ironic. He was a man preoccupied by past crimes. Indeed, he lived in fear of his own children being kidnapped. Few white people could better understand the existential terror of Indigenous parents. But there was no room in his heart for the past when it came to the mass theft of black kids. This wasn't ancient history, either. Members of the Stolen Generations were still alive to witness his indifference.

*

That winter, the Queensland Liberal and National parties merged. The Nationals had never recovered from the reputational damage of the Fitzgerald Inquiry. Post-Howard, the Liberal Party brand in Queensland was strong. But they were broke. The Nationals offered them assets and members. Peter Dutton had endorsed the amalgamation. Tony Abbott suggested that it could be replicated federally. George Brandis fought against the merger. He lost.

"The LNP's animating spirit is less Sir Robert Menzies than Sir Joh Bjelke-Petersen," wrote Brandis in 2023. Though in practice, Brandis was surprised to discover that the Nationals were less intolerant of Menzian moderates like him than certain conservatives in the Liberal Party.

After the merger, a top priority for LNP powerbrokers was locating a safe seat for Dutton. Dickson had undergone a redistribution. It was nominally Labor. So Dutton sought preselection for McPherson, a safe seat on the glitzy southern tip of the Gold Coast. He got glowing testimonials from "everyone except the Pope," including John Howard. According to a former female Liberal cabinet minister, safe seats were seen as a boys' club.

"There was a view in the Liberal Party that women were great in marginal seats, because they love talking to people," she says. "Really safe seats were for serious men who might potentially be treasurers and prime ministers." Tony Abbott publicly knighted Dutton as "a future leader of the party" and bemoaned his potential departure from parliament as a "tragedy."

Women were also gunning for preselection: Karen Andrews, chair of the McPherson division; and Minna Knight, a former adviser to Julie Bishop. Dutton held a grudge against Bishop for endorsing her old employee. His golden handshake turned into a PR disaster. "To some he's the messiah, to other's he's just another duplicitous polly," read a headline in *The Age*.

Dutton won the first two rounds of the preselection. Then he was defeated by Karen Andrews 75 to 59. Sources blamed the "hillbillies" of the National Party for derailing the coronation of Howard's favourite son. The LNP reneged on a promise to override the decision if he didn't win. Media reports suggested Dutton was eyeing off a parachute into Fisher or Fairfax on the Sunshine Coast. Labor dubbed him the Member for TBA (to be advised).

*

Malcolm Turnbull's leadership of the Liberal Party, which began in September 2008, was destined to end in tears. An Oxford-educated journalist, barrister and merchant banker from Sydney's eastern suburbs. The son-in-law of Tom Hughes, attorney-general under Fraser. Yet he was considered an impostor in the modern Liberal Party. Conservatives rallied around Tony Abbott. In December 2009, a spill was moved against Turnbull. The pretext for removal was his support of Labor's emissions trading scheme (ETS). Abbott won the leadership by a single vote.

"The right of the Liberal Party play by different rules," wrote Turnbull. "They threaten to blow the place up if they don't get their way … It is how a determined minority terrorises a majority into submission and then, over time, becomes the majority as more moderate or genuinely liberal members peel off."

The ensuing decade of leadership coups was viewed principally through the personalities of the protagonists involved. But there was much more to it. Labor's embrace of big business and deregulation – along with the calculated neutering of the trade union movement – didn't just collapse the social and ideological basis of left-wing politics down under. It also extinguished the unifying enemy that had kept such a motley crew of small-l liberals, big-c conservatives and agrarian protectionists glued together.

The post-war electoral coalitions of the major parties were designed for battles about capital and class, not gay marriage and climate change. In this new world, the Coalition-held seats of Wentworth and Kooyong did not really fit with Capricornia and Maranoa; just like the Labor-held seats of Sydney and Grayndler did not really fit with Hunter and Fowler. Hence the inability of both parties to govern without splitting their bases. And hence why conservative Liberals were relatively simpatico with the National Party.

Abbott ditched Turnbull's free-market approach to the ETS. He also removed the muzzle from conservatives on the subject of race. This spoke to parochial voters who didn't connect with the Rudd/Turnbull PC consensus. At the start of 2010, Abbott described Welcomes to Country as "tokenistic."

Liberal MP Wilson Tuckey called them a "farce". He complained about overweight Aboriginal dancers. Tuckey also called the 1967 referendum to remove discrimination of First Nations people from the constitution "the worst thing that's happened for Aboriginal people in history."

Dutton defended the right of Tuckey – an MP for thirty years – to remain unsilent. "I don't have any issue with what Wilson said, frankly, or his right to say it." On *Q&A*, Dutton said that Australians were getting "a little bit bored" by Welcomes to Country. No flood of compensation claims had come from the Apology. But he had zero regrets about boycotting the Apology.

Dutton wanted to put a stop to such navel-gazing. It was never just about the money. This was about power, and who speaks truth to it. This was about drawing a line in the history wars. "We should be wary of the return of the black armband view of history," he told the *Valley Star*. "The Coalition believes that, on balance, Australia's history is a cause for celebration."

Abbott was hailed by all and sundry as "unelectable". Something funny happened. A conservative in the hot seat of the Liberal Party magnified the cracks in Labor's fragile electoral coalition. Abbott wasn't popular. But he stoked the disillusionment of parochial voters in a way that Turnbull could never manage. Kevin Rudd panicked. He ditched the ETS.

In April 2010, Labor unveiled a plan to tax the super-profits of mining companies. Abbott warned that it would cause the overnight death of the mining industry. The Liberal scare campaign was temporarily undermined by a revelation: Dutton had purchased shares in BHP shortly after the policy announcement. "I bought them to put in the bottom drawer," he said.

In June, Rudd was removed in a brutal coup. His replacement, Julia Gillard, watered down the mining tax. At the August election Abbott picked up eleven predominantly outer-suburban and provincial electorates. The major parties ended up on the same number of seats: 72. Gillard deftly negotiated with the crossbench to secure minority government.

*

Tony Abbott turned the Gillard minority government into a daily witch trial. Dutton was curiously quiet. His job, as shadow health minister, was to muffle debate about a policy area that was unfavourable to the Liberals. At the 2013 election, Abbott promised to axe the tax and stop the boats. He was rewarded for an almost four-year campaign of everyday negativity. The Coalition won ninety seats in the lower house. Dutton became the health minister. "Dutton likely to play bad cop on health," reported journalist Samantha Maiden. She noted that he had come out of "witness protection" since the election.

Dutton became the figurehead for Abbott's biggest broken election promise: billions of dollars of funding cuts to health, and a plan to introduce a $7 GP co-payment. "We can't pretend, like Labor, that these services can be provided to everybody for free," said Dutton. "That would be the cheap and easy option." Voters turned against Abbott. There was a mutiny in the party room. Abbott lowered the proposed co-payment to $5, then dumped it altogether. Later, a survey by *Australian Doctor* magazine rated Peter Dutton the worst health minister in thirty-five years.

Abbott tried to rescue his flagging government. Scott Morrison was promoted from immigration to social services. Dutton was switched to immigration. Morrison had stopped the boats. Now Dutton wanted to stop the bikies. He announced a plan to allow border protection officials to carry guns. "If you're coming here harming Australians, ripping off our welfare system, committing serious crimes, then you're at the top of my list for deporting," wrote Dutton in a Facebook post.

On Australia Day 2015, Abbott decided to knight Prince Phillip. Less than a week later, the Queensland LNP lost thirty-six seats in the state election. First-term LNP premier Campbell Newman cited the knighthood as a factor. Leadership rumblings about Abbott led to a failed coup. It was time for Abbott and Dutton to break the glass containing emergency wedges.

In January 2015, hundreds of asylum seekers on Manus Island had gone on a hunger strike. Some stitched their lips together. One swallowed razor-blades. Riot police intervened. Dutton claimed that the asylum seekers were armed with weapons. This was contradicted by PNG officials. In

April, an armed mob stormed the refugee camp on Manus Island. Up to a hundred shots were fired. According to Dutton, the skirmish was caused by three asylum seekers trying to take a five-year-old boy into the compound. "There was a lot of angst around that," Dutton told Sky News. "I think there was concern about why the boy was being led, or for what purpose."

PNG denied Dutton's version of events. The boy was actually ten. He had been led into the compound a week earlier for fruit and water. The Good Friday riot had been caused by drunken soldiers and a soccer match gone wrong. "There are facts that I have that you don't," Dutton told journalists.

That autumn, Abbott sprang a proposal on cabinet. Dutton wanted the power to strip Australian citizenship from terrorism suspects. Even if they had no other citizenship. Even if they hadn't been charged with a crime. Decisions would be left to the sole discretion of the immigration minister, i.e. Peter Dutton. The changes were supported by Mike Pezzullo, the secretary of the Department of Immigration and Border Protection.

A fight erupted in cabinet. Senior moderates – Malcolm Turnbull, Julie Bishop, George Brandis and Christopher Pyne – predictably lined up against the plan. But even Barnaby Joyce was left gobsmacked by the overreach. "If we don't have enough evidence to charge someone with terrorism, how can we have enough evidence to cancel their citizenship?" asked Joyce. "That's the whole point," said Dutton. "We don't need as much evidence. It's an administrative decision and we don't have to justify it."

In trying to wedge Labor, Abbott and Dutton wedged themselves. The disagreement was promptly leaked to the newspapers. It added to the perception of disunity plaguing the government. Liberal MP Cory Bernardi – an arch-conservative – blasted the plan as "dangerous power creep." During tense meetings, Dutton and Pezzullo sneered at Turnbull for his resistance. "Dutton is a Queensland cop who has always found the third limb of government – the judiciary – an inconvenience," Brandis told Turnbull.

The historian Manning Clark described Australian public life as a contest between the enlargers and the punishers. Those with a craving for a freer way of being. And those clinging onto the authoritarian mindset of the convict colony. Dutton is a punisher. His desire to discipline the vulnerable comes from a visceral place. For John Howard, punishment was a means to power. For Dutton, power is a means to punishment.

*

Section 501 of Australia's *Migration Act* had been changed by the Coalition. This allowed the government to refuse or cancel a visa based on a vague "good character" test. Peter Dutton took full advantage. By his own admission, the immigration minister was still traumatised by the case of Sonny Graham, the Auckland-born Māori criminal who had raped a ten-year-old girl in suburban Brisbane. Now, with newfound executive power at his disposal, Dutton began deporting New Zealanders. "I sleep well at night knowing that deporting paedophiles from our shores mean[s] more Australian children won't fall victim to that paedophile," said Dutton in 2020.

On 31 August 2015, Joel Makaea, a 34-year-old father of four, was arrested and placed in immigration detention. The New Zealand–born bricklayer was expecting a child with his Australian partner. Makaea wasn't a paedophile. But he was sergeant-in-arms of the WA Rebels bikie gang. Membership of the Rebels wasn't illegal in Western Australia. It was still enough for Dutton to deport him. "Home You Go, Bro" read the headline of *The West Australian*. Makaea was held in immigration detention for over five months. His pregnant partner was forced to move houses and go on welfare. "They are doing this because of his tattoos and his size and because he looks intimidating," she said. "He doesn't know anyone back in New Zealand."

Makaea was paid a visit by a friend named Ngati Kanohi Te Eke Haapu, also known as Ko. Haapu was a decorated New Zealand war veteran. He had personally met and guarded Kiwi prime minister John Key in Afghanistan. Afterwards, Haapu settled in Perth and found employment on the mines. He fell in love with an Australian woman and became a stepfather to her child. The couple were expecting a child together.

Haapu had no criminal history whatsoever, but he was a member of the Rebels motorcycle gang. He had an inflammatory tattoo on his neck: FTP, an acronym for "Fuck the Police." After visiting Makaea, Haapu went for a sleep in his car. He woke up surrounded by taser-wielding police. Then, he was placed in solitary confinement at the same prison as Makaea. Dutton cancelled the Māori war hero's visa on the good character test. He was deported to New Zealand after four and a half months in immigration detention. This caused an uproar across the ditch.

"Australia has always had a much more frontier approach to justice than New Zealand, as the treatment of their Indigenous people has shown, and the current treatment of boat refugees continues to show," wrote Peter Dunne, the Minister for Internal Affairs in New Zealand's Key government.

Dutton insisted he had secret intelligence at his disposal contradicting the criticism. At least 60 per cent of the people deported to New Zealand between January 2015 and April 2018 were of Māori or Pacific Islander descent. Dutton described the deportations as Australia "taking out the trash."

*

Gaffe-prone Abbott was veering towards political self-destruction. Dutton accused Fairfax and ABC of running a "jihad" against the government. He briefly took the heat off the embattled PM. In September 2015, the bash brothers attended a meeting about Syrian refugees. They stood at the front of the room with Scott Morrison. The Middle Eastern community leaders were running late. "It's Cape York time," quipped Dutton, a joke about Aboriginals.

"What's this, mate?" asked Abbott.

"It's Cape York time!" said Dutton.

"I tell you we had a bit of that up in Port Moresby," said Abbott.

"Oh yeah," said Dutton, smirking.

"Yeah, yeah," said Abbott.

A sheepish Morrison tried to make polite conversation. Dutton interrupted with another pisstake. "Time doesn't mean anything when you're about to have water lapping at your door," said Dutton with a grin, as Abbott chuckled heartily. The punchline? Pacific Islanders were too busy getting wiped out by climate change. Abbott and Dutton didn't realise that their conversation was being recorded by microphones.

"There's a boom up there," muttered Morrison. The jokers froze. Dutton apologised, lukewarmly, for the "light-hearted discussion." He was just joshing.

The backlash overshadowed a more tangible example of Dutton's pitilessness towards Pacific Islanders. Junior Togatuki moved from Auckland to Western Sydney at the age of four. At the age of sixteen, he was arrested for armed robbery and assault. He spent seven years in prison. At the end of Togatuki's sentence, Dutton cancelled his visa. The schizophrenic young man of Samoan descent was placed in solitary confinement at a supermax prison, awaiting exile from his parents and siblings. "If I was to be deported back to New Zealand, I will be truly lost with myself," Togatuki wrote to Dutton. "I have no one there, no job, no home or a roof over my head. I'll lose all I have. I'll lose my family. I'll lose hope in life."

Togatuki's appeals were denied. A few hours after Dutton's joke about "Cape York time" and rising sea levels, Togatuki slashed his left wrist with a razor. He placed two crisis calls over the prison intercom. They were treated as false alarms by the guards, who were glued to an NRL semi-final. "God forgive me," Togatuki wrote on the wall in blood. "I'm sorry." Togatuki wanted to live. He tried to flood his cell as a cry for help. The guards ignored the water lapping underneath the locked door. Togatuki was found dead the next morning, eleven hours after the first crisis call.

Dutton was unrepentant. Shortly afterwards, the immigration minister deported a 56-year-old tetraplegic who had been living in Australia for thirty-six years. After breaking his neck, the man served twenty months in jail for self-medicating with painkillers. Two days before release, his visa was cancelled. The wheelchair-user spent four months in a detention centre. Then he was sent back to Auckland with $200 and a voucher for accommodation.

Publicly, Dutton was unflappable. Privately, he showed more discretion. That spring, a 27-year-old French tourist was detained by immigration officials at Adelaide airport. She was planning to work unlawfully as an au pair for Callum MacLachlan, a wealthy pastoralist. MacLachlan's family had previously donated $150,000 to the state and federal Liberals. His cousin was Gillon McLachlan, the AFL CEO. His uncle, Ian, had been defence minister in the Howard government. Gillon lobbied Dutton's office to liberate his cousin's au pair. Dutton promptly intervened.

"I have decided that as a discretionary and humanitarian act to an individual with ongoing needs, it is in the interests of Australia as a humane and generous society to grant this person a visitor visa," Dutton wrote. Six months later, Callum MacLachlan's father donated $50,000 to the South Australian Liberal Party.

It wasn't the lone example of Dutton showing rapid-fire compassion towards European au pairs. He also intervened in the case of an Italian at Brisbane Airport. She came to work as a babysitter for Russell Keag, Dutton's old colleague in the Queensland police. Within hours, Dutton had overturned the advice of his own department to grant her a visa.

Tony Abbott lost thirty Newspolls in a row. Malcolm Turnbull launched a leadership coup. He won by 54 votes to 44. Abbott was a wrecker of epic proportions. He wrecked Kevin Rudd. He wrecked Julia Gillard. Then he wrecked himself. Government proved beyond his undeniable yet one-dimensional skillset. Abbott slunk to the backbench, determined to wreck Turnbull. Dutton remained immigration minister. But he was infuriated by the coup. "I still think about those awful events in mid-September 2015 and the cruel fate which should never have befallen [Abbott]," he wrote in 2023.

Dutton filled the vacuum of gaffes. In November 2015, South Australian MP Jamie Briggs went on an official government trip to Hong Kong. Briggs reportedly told a 26-year-old DFAT staffer that she had "piercing eyes," before attempting to kiss her on the cheek in a crowded bar. The story was recounted by Samantha Maiden for News Corp. Dutton drafted a text message to Jamie Briggs calling the senior female journalist "a mad fucking witch." Alas, Dutton accidentally sent the message to Maiden. This was awkward for Dutton, given that he had called for the sacking of Peter Slipper as speaker in 2012, following the publication of sexist text messages.

Turnbull refused to sack Dutton. The PM needed a right-wing headkicker to counteract the renaissance of Pauline Hanson. Following a stint in prison, Hanson had spent the previous decade rehabilitating herself on breakfast TV and *Dancing with the Stars*. Now she was running for the Senate. Dutton was given free rein on talkback radio and *Sky After Dark* to stem the potential defection of Coalition voters to One Nation, especially in Queensland. The Greens called for Australia to increase its refugee intake to 50,000 people a year. It was a slam dunk for Dutton. "What on God's earth are these people suggesting about 50,000 people being taken from every hellhole of the world?" Paul Murray asked the immigration minister.

"They won't be numerate or literate in their own language, let alone English," said Dutton. "These people would be taking Australian jobs. There's no doubt about that. For many of them that would be unemployed, they would languish in unemployment queues and on Medicare."

Opposition leader Bill Shorten was proposing to cut the capital gains discount for property investors from 50 per cent to 25 per cent, and to restrict negative gearing to newly built properties. Dutton called the modest changes "a housing tax." The immigration minister had skin in the game. *The Australian* estimated he was worth "at least $10 million – perhaps as much as $20 million." In 2014, the Duttons had bought a beachfront mansion on the Gold Coast for $2.325 million. Neighbours included mining tycoon Clive Palmer and media heir Ryan Stokes. They also owned a villa at Tangalooma Resort on Moreton Island and two apartments: one in inner-city Brisbane and one in Canberra. "The economy will come to a shuddering halt, and I think the stock market will crash," said Dutton of Labor's tax proposals.

Bill Shorten fought fire with fire. He ran the mother of all scare campaigns about Medicare, largely based on the actions of Dutton as health minister. At the 2016 election, Turnbull secured a one-seat majority. He was criticised by Liberals for not being negative enough. For Dutton, it was the worst campaign in Liberal Party history. "Malcolm is charming and affable but he doesn't have a political bone in his body," said Dutton in 2018.

After the election, Dutton's wife, Kirilly, bought a shopping centre in Townsville. Dutton forgot to declare this on his registry of assets. What was a shopping centre in the grand scheme of things? He was a busy man.

One Nation gained 4.29 per cent of the national vote and four seats in the Senate. Then the election of Donald Trump – so soon after Brexit – sent a tremor through Australia's major parties. Especially with a resurrected Pauline Hanson toasting the victory over a glass of champagne from the front lawns of Parliament House. "Why I'm celebrating is that I can see people now around the world are saying: *We've had enough of the establishment. We're sick and tired of the elites,*" she said.

Along with a royal commission into climate change, Hanson wanted to abolish the Family Law Court. It would be replaced by a tribunal of "people from mainstream Australia." The idea was almost identical to the one Dutton had pursued as a backbencher. Migrants from East Asia had been replaced by Arabs as Hanson's prime target. The intake of Muslim refugees should be halted; the burqa banned in public places; surveillance cameras installed at mosques. "Pauline Hanson has some good points to make," said Dutton.

Turnbull and Dutton settled into a good cop, bad cop routine. They attempted to straddle both sides of a fraying electoral coalition. Turnbull extolled innovation to blue-ribbon Liberal seats. Over the next two years, Dutton flung red meat to the base with the dexterity of a teppanyaki chef. During an interview with Andrew Bolt, he claimed that Malcolm Fraser erred by letting in so many migrants from war-torn countries in the 1970s. Labor pounced. In parliament, Dutton was pressed to identify Fraser's mistakes.

"The advice I have is that out of the last thirty-three people who have been charged with terrorist-related offences in this country, twenty-two of those people are from second- and third-generation Lebanese-Muslim background," said Dutton. In other words, Fraser made a mistake letting in the Lebanese. Not the Christians. Just the Muslims. Dutton was accused of racism. His inflammatory statements were framed as gaffes: a right-wing redneck letting his mask slip. They were anything but accidental. Calling a journalist "a mad fucking witch" was a blooper. Race-baiting was a political tactic. Outrage from Labor, the Greens and Twitter users was a key performance indicator.

*

In January 2017, Malcolm Turnbull made a phone call to Donald Trump. Turnbull had previously cut a deal with Barack Obama to export up to 1250 refugees from Nauru and Manus Island to the United States. Trump had just announced a travel ban on Muslims. He wanted to dump the deal. Turnbull reassured Trump they weren't terrorists. He insisted that if these people had arrived by plane – and not boat – they would now be in Australia. Turnbull offered to trade the boat people for undesirables from America.

"We would rather take a not very attractive guy that helps you out than to take a Nobel Peace Prize winner that comes by boat," said Turnbull.

The president was flummoxed. It took a leaked call with Trump to exemplify the absurdity of Australia's border policies. He demonstrated more critical thinking skills about boat people than much of the Australian media. "What is the thing with boats?" asked Trump. "Why do you discriminate against boats? No, I know, they come from certain regions. I get it."

Trump begrudgingly agreed to honour the deal. Fifty-two asylum seekers from Nauru and Manus Island passed the extensive vetting process to live in the United States. The refugees were genuine enough for Trump, but not for Dutton.

"They're economic refugees," he told old mate Ray Hadley on 2GB. "They got on a boat, paid a people smuggler a lot of money, and somebody once said to me that we've got the world's biggest collection of Armani jeans and handbags up on Nauru waiting for people to collect it when they depart."

Dutton kept his foot on their throats. The boats had stopped. But Dutton was just getting started. In the lucky country, there was a direct correlation between how low he would go and how high he could climb.

*

The Hard Right faction formed a recovery meeting for conservative survivors of Turnbull's coup. Dutton hosted the lunches in a room beside his ministerial office. It included old fogeys such as Eric Abetz and Kevin Andrews; new turks such as Angus Taylor, Tony Pasin, Zed Seselja, Michael Sukkar and Andrew Hastie; and Tony Abbott, the vengeful ex-PM. Upon arrival, attendees paid cash to one of Dutton's staffers. Then they tucked into a succulent Chinese meal at a table made of timber from a monkey pod tree. Hence the nickname for this political guerrilla group: The Monkey Pod.

"Shit, it was strange," says a temporary member of the Monkey Pod. The meetings were a safe space for climate change denialism. Dutton enabled it. But he was tight-lipped, allowing the other members to rant and rave, before summing up the conversation with a succinct one-liner. "It didn't feel like a Liberal Party meeting at all," says the ex-member, who quit going after a few Chinese lunches. "Very right-wing. *We'll reclaim the good old days at some stage. We just need to wait patiently.* That was the vibe I got."

Dutton facilitated unrest in the Monkey Pod, while publicly defending Turnbull. With Mathias Cormann, Dutton formed a "praetorian guard" around the prime minister. Turnbull ignored warnings from Julie Bishop, Christopher Pyne and George Brandis that he was being double-crossed. Dutton and Cormann warned Turnbull not to trust Bishop and Brandis.

"I told Malcolm that the day would come where Dutton would come after him," George Brandis tells me. "And he just laughed at me. He said: 'don't be stupid; as if [Dutton] could be prime minister.'"

On the subject of race, Dutton was at one with Abbott and the Monkey Pod. On the subject of sexuality, his social conservatism was tested. Dutton was inherently opposed to gay marriage. In March 2017, thirty Australian CEOs signed an open letter imploring Turnbull to get it legislated. Dutton told the CEOs to "stick to their knitting." He singled out Qantas CEO Alan Joyce – an openly gay man – for a special serve. "Alan Joyce, the individual, is perfectly entitled to campaign for and spend his hard-earned money on any issue he sees fit, but don't do it in the official capacity and with shareholders' money," said Dutton to raucous applause at an LNP conference in Cairns.

As prime minister, Abbott had sabotaged a free vote on gay marriage by hosting an unconventional joint party vote with the Nationals. His compromise policy was to stage a plebiscite if re-elected. Now that Turnbull was leader, the Mad Monk waged war on gay marriage. The debate was suffocating Turnbull. Dutton proposed going around parliament with a postal vote conducted by the Australian Bureau of Statistics. He took the lead internally, while Turnbull feigned scepticism of the idea. "Mathias and I worked with colleagues on the postal plebiscite," said Dutton. "Without that, Malcolm would never have survived that issue and he knew it."

Dutton tried to have his cake and eat it too. He criticised the political correctness of the Yes campaign. American rapper Macklemore was planning to sing "One Love" before the NRL Grand Final, six weeks before the postal survey. "I don't think Australian parents taking their kids to the footy want political messages down their throat," said Dutton. "Presumably two songs will be played: one for gay marriage, and one against gay marriage."

Dutton didn't specify which anti-gay marriage song might be sung. The naysayer was obfuscating his collaboration with the woke agenda of Labor; the moderate faction of the Liberals; and corporate Australia. Trevor Evans had volunteered for Dutton in his 2001 campaign against Cheryl Kernot. In 2016, Evans became Queensland's first openly gay federal MP. "My very firm view is that marriage equality was only achieved in 2017 in Australia because of the productive role Peter Dutton played," said Evans.

Nationwide, 61.6 per cent voted Yes to same-sex marriage; 38.4 per cent voted No. In Dutton's seat of Dickson, 65.2 per cent of locals voted Yes. Dutton wasn't one of them. He voted No. But sitting on a margin of 1.6 per cent, he took heed of his constituents and voted Yes to the legislation. Abbott and Morrison abstained. "I am not a Bible-basher or some right-wing extremist, but that suits how the left want to define me," said Dutton in 2018.

This was the much-trumpeted pragmatic side of Dutton. There was something in it for him. He judged – correctly – that Middle Australia had mostly moved on from outdated attitudes about LGBTIQA+ people, in a way that they hadn't with Indigenous people and asylum seekers. The postal survey was an electoral and professional calculation, not a moral one.

*

Turnbull repaid Dutton with a new super-ministry: Home Affairs. The merger was opposed by the AFP and ASIO. Their concerns were shared by George Brandis, the attorney-general and Dutton's ongoing foe. Dutton wanted to oust Brandis so his ally Mathias Cormann could become leader of the Senate. "It is for the attorney-general always to defend the rule of law," said Brandis in 2018, "sometimes from political colleagues who fail to understand it."

Home Affairs was the brainchild of Mike Pezzullo. In 2013, the idea had been rejected by Tony Abbott, but was beloved by Scott Morrison. Now Pezzullo and Dutton twisted Turnbull's arm. Pezzullo formed an inappropriately close relationship with Scott Briggs, a confidant of Turnbull and Morrison. Pezzullo was meant to be an apolitical public servant. But throughout 2017, he secretly lobbied Briggs for the scalp of Brandis.

"Home Affairs is going well except Agd [Brandis's department] needs to be put to the sword," Pezzullo messaged Scott Briggs via WhatsApp.

"Haha," responded Briggs. "Will pass it on."

That year, Pezzullo detailed the justification for the concentration of so much power in the hands of one man. His speech referenced *The Lord of the Rings*. Australians were like hobbits. Presumably, this made Pezzullo Gandalf and Dutton Frodo. "The state has to increasingly embed itself – not majestically, sitting at the apex of society, dispensing justice, but … in a seamless and largely invisible fashion," said Pezzullo.

Turnbull gave Pezzullo and Dutton what they wanted. In Home Affairs, Dutton retained responsibility for immigration and border control. He also seized responsibility for national security from the attorney-general; transport security from the infrastructure minister; counterterrorism and cybersecurity from the PM; and multicultural affairs from the social services minister. Dutton became perhaps the most powerful minister in Australian history. He was the spectre haunting George Brandis's retirement speech. "Powerful elements of right-wing politics have abandoned both liberalism's concern for the rights of the individual and conservatism's respect for institutions, in favour of a belligerent, intolerant populism," said Brandis.

Dutton declared war on public institutions; the rule of law; civic liberties; and the fourth estate of media. He unquestionably benefited from the politicisation of the bureaucracy. But what was it all for? There was very little evidence of Dutton being competent at or particularly passionate about his primary job: the development and implementation of public policy.

"Do you think Home Affairs has been well administered?" Turnbull asks me. He lived to regret the unprecedented power he surrendered to Dutton. "You could blame that all on Pezzullo. But Peter was the minister."

*

In September 2017, Home Affairs awarded a contract for running detention centres on Manus Island to an inexperienced security company called Paladin. It was registered to a beach shack at the end of a dirt road on Kangaroo Island. According to Mike Pezzullo, there were no other options. He used special powers to award Paladin the contract without a competitive tender process. According to the *Australian Financial Review*, Paladin was charging taxpayers $450,000 a year – over $1600 a day per refugee on Manus Island. This didn't include food. Refugees were expected to cook and to wash their own clothes. Local employees were paid roughly $2 an hour.

Between May 2018 and October 2019, Paladin was fined a total of $5.8 million for 5484 separate "performance failures." Paladin transferred over $3 million to a PNG politician to facilitate visa approvals for staff. In total, Paladin received $532 million from the Australian government. The majority owner, Craig Thrupp, was a former soldier. Thrupp's mother was an employee in the Home Affairs department. Her partner, Dermot Casey, had been a senior figure in the immigration department. He provided advice on Paladin's "community engagement strategy." Not long after winning the original contract, Thrupp gifted his mum $1.2 million. "I did not 'pay' my mother anything," said Thrupp. "I did transfer her some amounts as an individual. I am her son and I was supporting my mother."

When eventually quizzed about the contract, Dutton stonewalled the media, claiming he needed to protect a geopolitical relationship. The minister denied that he had any oversight of the decision, but defended the premise. "There are very few people who can deliver services in the middle of nowhere on an island that is so remote," Dutton told Sky News in 2019.

It wasn't the only dubious agreement. In July 2017, Home Affairs awarded a contract to operate detention centres on Nauru to Canstruct International. As with Paladin on Manus Island, there was no competitive tender process. In 2023, the repercussions of this decision were investigated by Nine Newspapers and *60 Minutes* for their "Home Truths" series.

Canstruct International was owned by the Murphys, a wealthy Queensland construction family. They had no prior experience running detention centres. Their new company – Canstruct International – had "$8 in working capital." Home Affairs commissioned a financial assessment by KPMG. The consulting firm was directed to assess the Murphys' construction company instead. It was found to have a "moderate to high financial risk."

Over the next five years, Canstruct International received $1.82 billion from Home Affairs. Millions of dollars were channelled into contracts with businesses owned by Nauruan politicians. $435,000 ended up in the personal bank account of the Nauruan president. The AFP later launched an investigation into the lawfulness of these activities. By September 2021, only 107 asylum seekers were left on Nauru, but Canstruct still employed 428 staff. The company was getting paid over $3 million a year per refugee.

Between 2017 and 2020, the Murphys and their associates made eleven donations to the LNP, totalling $47,500. Peter Dutton met with Canstruct executives three times at LNP dinners, including CEO Rory Murphy. The shadow attorney-general, Mark Dreyfus, probed the donations. "This looks like yet another example of the Liberal Party using public money like it's Liberal Party money and helping out their mates," said Dreyfus.

While presiding over reckless spending on questionable contracts, Dutton starved resources from compliance officers who prevented visa fraud. In 2022, Nine Newspapers and *60 Minutes* exposed the systematic rorting of Australia's migration system. Foreigners on student visas were treated as modern-day indentured labourers. Vulnerable women were shunted across the country and kept as sex slaves. Provided they arrived by plane and not boat, drug smugglers remained free by making bogus asylum applications.

Labor launched an inquiry. It was headed by Christine Nixon, Victoria's former top cop. Nine Newspapers and *60 Minutes* further exposed the failures of Home Affairs. Albanian gangsters had been running riot in Adelaide. Dutton's tunnel vision for punishing refugees – at any cost – blinded him to the criminals and slaves arriving by plane. "We were told that the department's energy went into the boats," Christine Nixon told Nine.

Dutton was great at punishing asylum seekers. Great at conveying strength to swinging voters in marginal seats. Great at cultivating relationships with conservative commentators. Great at destroying internal obstacles to his irrepressible ambitions. But he was not so great at running a government department with transparency and integrity. Nor at protecting Australians from international drug and sex trafficking syndicates. His bad cop act was a triumph of style over substance.

As the right came to terms with gay marriage, Dutton reminded them he was the keeper of the flame. Over the 2017–18 summer, Melbourne was beset by a crime wave. Shock jocks whipped up hysteria about Sudanese youth. "The reality is, you know, that people [in Melbourne] are scared to go out to restaurants of a night-time," Dutton told Chris Kenny on 2GB, "because they're followed home by these gangs. Home invasions. And cars are stolen. And we just need to call it for what it is. Of course it's African gang violence."

Dutton couldn't blame African gangs on Fraser. Most asylum seekers from Sudan had arrived in Australia under Howard. So he blamed the crime wave on Daniel Andrews, the Labor premier of Victoria. Dutton accused Victorian courts of becoming infected by left-wing political correctness. He called for the youthful wrongdoers and their families to be deported. "If they aren't prepared to send their kids to school," said Dutton. "If they have ten- and twelve-year-old kids wandering the streets at night committing these offences, then frankly they don't belong in Australian society."

Dutton had a soft spot for some Africans. The South African government was attempting to redistribute farmland from whites to blacks. It was the kind of reverse-dispossession that kept Australian farmers awake at night during native title debates. News Corp columnist Miranda Devine criticised Dutton for prioritising Muslim refugees above "our oppressed white, Christian, industrious, rugby and cricket-playing Commonwealth cousins from South Africa, who would integrate seamlessly."

In 2018, Dutton flagged fast-tracking the refugee applications of white South Africans. The South African government demanded a retraction, accusing Dutton of misinformation. Australian foreign minister Julie Bishop vowed that the applications of refugees would continue to be judged on need, not skin colour. Dutton went on the Ray Hadley show. "I mean some of the crazy lefties at the ABC and on *The Guardian* … can express concern and draw mean cartoons about me and all the rest of it," said Dutton. "They don't realise how completely dead they are to me … If people think that I'm going to cower or take a backward step because of their nonsense, fabricated, fake news criticism, then they've got another thing coming."

Malcolm Turnbull lost thirty Newspolls in a row. This had been his justification for the coup against Abbott. The Monkey Pod went into overdrive. They waged war on Turnbull over the National Energy Guarantee (NEG). Speculation swirled that Abbott's masterplan was to destroy Turnbull and let someone else – i.e. Dutton – take the fall at the 2019 election. Then Abbott would be miraculously resurrected as Liberal leader.

Dutton denied that he was a stalking horse for Abbott. He had long been disarmingly candid about the fact he desperately wanted to be leader. "Of course I want to be prime minister," Dutton told *Guardian Australia*.

Seemingly everyone was aware of this. Apart, that is, from Turnbull. The PM had chortled at George Brandis's direct warnings that he was being stalked. Turnbull seemed to sincerely believe that Dutton – perhaps the most power-hungry person in the Australian parliament – would be happy to continue playing second fiddle. "Dutton had never struck me as being so self-delusional and narcissistic as to imagine that he could successfully lead the Liberal Party," wrote Turnbull in his autobiography, *A Bigger Picture*.

The bumbling leadership tussle between Turnbull and Dutton epitomised a stalemate between the Old Liberals, urbane and highly educated, and the New Liberals, provincial and contemptuous of the knowledge class. Dutton was still nursing a grudge against the fashionable compassion of the blabbermouthed barristers who represented the criminals he had attempted to keep off the streets. "Malcolm saw the Liberal Party as a vehicle to being prime minister," Dutton would later tell Niki Savva. "He was a barrister who could argue a brief for either side."

The tipping point came in the Sunshine State. A byelection in Longman was viewed by Queensland Coalition MPs as a simulation of the next election. The LNP's primary vote plummeted by 9.4 per cent. One Nation's primary vote rose to 15.91 per cent. Labor regained the seat. Turnbull blamed the LNP. The LNP blamed Turnbull, that smug southerner, for opening up the floodgates to One Nation. LNP president Gary Spence directed Queenslanders to support Dutton in any leadership spill. Ray Hadley staged a daily campaign for listeners to contact Liberal MPs demanding the removal of Turnbull. On Thursday, 17 August, Dutton called in for his weekly appearance. Hadley berated him for remaining loyal to Turnbull.

"There comes a time in history where you've got to have the bottle, and another part of your anatomy, to stand up for yourself, mate," said Hadley. In other words: are you a man or a mouse? By that afternoon, Hadley was back on the air for an emergency announcement. The shock jock had been making some calls and crunching the numbers. He confidently predicted that Dutton would "100 per cent" challenge for the leadership.

The following week, Turnbull delayed the NEG, attempting to avert a leadership spill. Overnight, word reached Turnbull that the LNP MP Luke Howarth had been openly blowing up about the need for him to go. Howarth was an ex–pest control man from outer-suburban Brisbane who was married to Dutton's cousin. The next day, Dutton took a seat next to Tony Abbott in the party-room meeting. Turnbull made a speech about the need for unity. Luke Howarth dramatically leapt to his feet. "You should resign," he cried.

Turnbull called Dutton's bluff. He declared the leadership positions vacant. It was an ambush: the Dutton camp didn't have the numbers yet. Turnbull nominated. There was a pregnant pause. Abbott whacked Dutton on the knee. He stood up and buttoned his blazer. The ballot papers were distributed and counted. Turnbull defeated Dutton 48 to 35. Dutton was just seven votes short of being the prime minister. "He is dead," thought Dutton.

Turnbull and Dutton shook hands. Afterwards, they had a private meeting with Cormann. According to Dutton, Turnbull offered him the deputy leadership. According to Turnbull, Cormann demanded the demotion of Julie Bishop as a peace offering. In Turnbull's version of events, he asked why they'd want to knock off Bishop, one of the party's great electoral assets. "Because people think she's Malcolm Turnbull in a skirt," said Dutton.

Dutton told Turnbull he was going to keep coming until the numbers swung. But counting numbers had never been his strong suit. Hadley – his unofficial campaign manager – was no match for a well-oiled moderate machine. Nor was Dutton helped by an endorsement from Pauline Hanson. "If Dutton gets up, we would want to talk to him," said Queensland One Nation leader Steve Dickson. "He has a similar belief system to ours."

Dutton outlined a populist manifesto to beat the Labor Party at the 2019 election. Under him, there would be a crackdown on Chinese investment. Migration would be cut by an undefined amount. This would address the traffic congestion and lack of infrastructure in the outer suburbs of the capital cities. "I think we do have to cut the numbers back," he said.

Dutton was also open to withdrawing from the Paris Agreement. Last but not least, he wanted to exempt the electricity bills of Australian families from the GST, a 10 per cent cut. Politically, this might have been a hit. But it would have cost the budget $32 billion over ten years. "Peter wants to be prime minister," Turnbull tells me. "So he will say and do what he needs to get there. But he is not the sharpest tool in the shed."

On Thursday morning, Dutton visited Turnbull to demand another spill. Turnbull warned Dutton he was possibly ineligible to sit in parliament, due to the constitutional implications of his childcare investments. This pressing eligibility issue had escaped Turnbull's to-do list until now.

It was a delicious twist of fate. Dutton's road to the top was blocked by an inner-city barrister, his most hated mishmash of geography and occupation. Star of the Spycatcher case. Kerry Packer's personal solicitor. Turnbull deployed all that legal pedantry and experience dealing with high-stakes negotiations to sabotage the dream of a phlegmatic Queenslander.

Et tu, Brute? Nah, mate. Just Dutts.

Turnbull announced that he would quit parliament if replaced as leader, forcing a byelection. He demanded a list with forty-three signatures – a majority – before another spill would be called. It would only be held after receiving advice about Dutton's eligibility from the solicitor-general. All of this planted seeds of doubt in the minds of those tossing up a vote for Dutton.

The Monkey Pod believed they could strongarm their colleagues into signing the petition, especially the women. Dutton needed fewer Sukkars and Seseljas; more Christopher Pynes, the South Australian moderate Liberal. "Mate, you should buy the Dame Edna Everage franchise when Barry Humphries is finished with it," Dutton used to light-heartedly mock Pyne.

Unbeknown to the Monkey Pod, one of their walls led to Pyne's office. He eavesdropped on "the most hopeless" coup of his career, while humming "Rock and Roll Heaven" by the Righteous Brothers. "They were an amateur hour operation," wrote Pyne. "It was like open mic at 'the Graham Richardson School of Whatever It Takes' karaoke night."

Pyne made a ruthless adjudication. Turnbull was cactus. It was now a three-way race between Dutton, Bishop and Morrison. Bishop was the most popular Liberal politician among the general public. She was the one alternative prime minister who might have prevented the looming teal revolution, and the rejection of the Coalition by Western Australia. "In hindsight, we should've stuck with J-Bish," a moderate MP tells me.

Morrison was the protégé of Brian Houston. He kept a boat-shaped trophy on his desk, etched with the phrase: "I Stopped These." He later waved around a lump of coal in parliament. But unlike Dutton, Morrison was a chameleon. He could reinvent himself. Dutton was utterly himself: a tough-nut conservative from Queensland. "Peter as leader would have been political suicide in Melbourne," a then cabinet minister from Victoria tells me.

If the moderates swung behind Bishop, Morrison would be knocked out in the first round. However, Dutton might win. The moderates made a deal with the devil: Morrison. Turnbull accepted that the game was up. Julie Bishop and Scott Morrison officially threw their hats into the ring. On Friday morning, the petition finally hit forty-three signatures. Dutton delivered the petition to Turnbull. Turnbull stymied him one last time for luck, claiming that he wanted to verify the legitimacy of the signatures.

A spill was called. The motion to declare the leadership vacant passed 45–40. "This is a farce," muttered Turnbull. He quit. Dutton, Bishop and Morrison stood for the leadership. Bishop was knocked out in the first round with 11 votes. Dutton had 38 votes. Morrison sat on 36 votes. The second ballot was counted. The whips re-entered the room. What went through

Dutton's head? All of that pain and rage and patience for *this*. A moment of grace became available. He was so close to Howard's crown. Now, it was a race between him and a bloke he absolutely loathed: Morrison.

Power slipped through Dutton's outstretched fingers like sand. Morrison triumphed, 45 to 40. After all that subterfuge, Dutton was just three votes short of being prime minister. Always the headkicker, never the king.

Peter Dutton was cleared of eligibility issues. It was too late. Scott Morrison kept him as Home Affairs minister, but Dutton lost immigration. He was under siege. Left-wing advocacy group GetUp was flooding Dickson with anti-Dutton volunteers and advertising. A former Liberal staffer named Gerard Benedet started Advance Australia, a right-wing GetUp. It raised money to defend Dutton. Satirical superheroes named "Captain GetUp" and "Freddie Foreign Money" were unleashed on the streets of Dickson.

Labor preselected a star candidate: Ali France. Six years earlier, France was pushing her four-year-old son, Zac, in a stroller through a shopping centre. A car driven by an 88-year-old man veered towards them. France took the full brunt of the impact. Zac suffered burns to the legs but was otherwise unharmed. France's femoral artery had been severed. Her left leg was amputated above the knee. She was left with crippling PTSD.

"I would see the frozen face of the man who had hit me everywhere – in my dreams, in my house, outside my house," she wrote. "Fear completely engulfed me. Fear became a bigger disability for me than losing my leg."

France's guardian angel turned out to be a Sydney surgeon named Dr Munjed Al Muderis. In 1999, the Iraqi doctor arrived on Christmas Island via boat. The following year, Australia accepted him as a refugee. Now, Dr Al Muderis implanted a titanium rod into Ali France's leg. It connected her prosthetic to the bone. She could walk again. The experience crystallised France's opposition to Australia's offshore detention policy.

By 2019, France was working in Dickson at a charity for palliative-care patients. She lived in the neighbouring seat of Brisbane. Her suburban house was seven minutes from Dickson. It had been specially renovated to provide disability access. "I have searched high and low for a wheelchair accessible house in the electorate [of Dickson] but anyone who has a disability like mine will know that it is almost impossible to find suitable homes," France told *The Australian*.

France pointed out she owned just one property. She couldn't couch-surf at a mate's place for the election. Dutton was remorseless. He saw another Kernot in the making. "There are plenty of people with disability living in Dickson," said Dutton. "A lot of people have raised this with me. I think they are quite angry that Ms France is using her disability as an excuse."

Tanya Plibersek called Dutton "pea-hearted." She argued that Dutton was spending more time at his mansion on the Gold Coast than in Dickson. Morrison didn't buy into the fight – perhaps because he had gained preselection for Cook while living fifty minutes away in Bronte. Dutton doubled down. "Dickson constituents believe Ms France's refusal to live in the electorate, even if she won the seat, is more about her enjoying the inner-city lifestyle," said his spokeswoman.

The next day, Dutton apologised to Ali France via a tweet. It was trademark Dutton. Generate outrage, then kind of say sorry, without outlining what he was sorry about. In the aftermath, ABC Radio hosted a debate between Dutton and France at the Pine Rivers Bowls Club. Dutton wore a pink tie to show his softer side. "Ali has said before that she's ashamed to be an Australian," Dutton told the punters at the bowls club.

The truth was a bit more ambiguous. In 2016, France retweeted an op-ed in *The New York Times* titled: "I Am Ashamed to Be Australian." It was by a journalist covering conditions on Nauru. France had since deleted the tweet. At the local bowlo, Dutton promised to defend Australia's borders. The crowd erupted in cheers. "I've represented Australia twice in sport," said France. "I've won three gold medals … It's really unfair saying that."

This wasn't Dutton's first rodeo. Going so hard for the jugular of a disabled woman – a heroic mother, no less – might seem like a counterintuitive way to win a marginal seat. But Dutton wanted to make France seem vulnerable; fragile; too large-hearted for a bastard of a world. It was a delicate balancing act. Dutton also needed to appear at least loosely human to outer-suburban mums. So he brought out the big guns. News Corp ran a cover story across the country of Dutton cuddling his wife, Kirilly.

"MY PETE'S NO MONSTER," read the headline. The subtitle: "... but the sickos who threaten our kids are." The Peter she knew was a cricket tragic. "He's a really good man and he's not a monster," said Kirilly Dutton.

It was panic stations. According to most of the media, Scott Morrison was destined for defeat. The Opposition was already divvying up the ministries and preparing its staff for government. Old Labor leaders turned their hatchets on the Coalition instead of each other. "I've never seen any public figure as mean or mean-spirited as Peter Dutton," Paul Keating told the ABC. "Those electors in Dickson have a chance to drive a political stake through his dark political heart and I hope they do."

Morrison pulled off a miracle win. Abbott lost Warringah to Zali Steggall. But Dutton defeated Ali France with a 2.95 per cent swing. At his victory party, Dutton was unusually jubilant. He beamed at the true believers. "I want to quote a former prime minister," said Dutton. "His name was Paul Keating. And the quote was: 'this is the sweetest victory of all'."

*

Labor's shock defeat at the 2019 election exposed the faultlines of modern Australian politics: education and geography. In the twenty seats with the highest proportion of university graduates, Labor achieved a 3.78 per cent swing in its favour. In the twenty seats with the lowest proportion of university graduates, Labor suffered a 4.22 per cent swing against it. The ALP's ruthless campaign review elucidated the group of voters whom Peter Dutton would eventually identify as the new Forgotten People. It read:

> Labor lost support amongst its traditional base of lower-income working people. Economically vulnerable workers living in outer-metropolitan, regional and rural Australia have lost trust in politicians and political institutions. Not only are they alienated from the political process, they are too busy working and caring for their families to be concerned with issues they consider irrelevant to their lives. Indeed, they are often resentful of the attention progressive political parties give at their expense to minority groups and to what is

> nowadays called identity politics. The media often described these types of voters as "Howard's Battlers" during the 1990s and 2000s – until he inflicted WorkChoices on them. Today, the Coalition seeks to label them Scott Morrison's "Quiet Australians." They are the same demographic that swung against the Democrats towards Donald Trump in 2016 and who are ditching progressive parties around the western world.

This demographic was populated by working-class men *and* women across the country, not just cashed-up tradies and Queensland coalminers. There just happened to be a lot more of them up north. Morrison was a genius at connecting with them through crisp images and folksy soundbites. But Dutton detected their deepest fears better than anyone. Not because he was a genius or a psychic, but because he was also afraid of change.

After the 2019 election, Dutton kept cultivating his reputation for racial division. He wanted to repeal the Medevac legislation, which allowed refugees to receive urgent medical attention in Australia. Dutton claimed that women were faking rapes so they could receive abortions on Australian shores, before seeking legal injunctions preventing return to Nauru.

"Some people are trying it on," Dutton told Sky News.

Dutton had a bee in his bonnet about a Sri Lankan couple named Nades and Priya Nadesalingam. Nades arrived by boat in 2012. He claimed persecution due to being a member of the Tamil Tigers army. Priya arrived by boat in 2013. She claimed to have witnessed her ex-husband be burned alive. Nades and Priya were given temporary visas. They met, fell in love and settled in the Central Queensland town of Biloela. Nades got a job at the abattoir. A daughter named Kopika was born in 2015, and another named Tharnicaa followed in 2017. The family was embraced by the community.

In March 2018, at 5 a.m., Border Force officials staged a raid on their home. They were accompanied by Serco guards and Queensland police. This was under the authority of Dutton's super-ministry. Nades' and Priya's visas had just expired. Kopika was two. Tharnicaa was nine months old. Without warning, the family was whisked to a detention centre in Melbourne for deportation. "It's been very clear to them at every turn that they were not going to stay in Australia, and they still had children," Dutton told Ray Hadley. "We see that overseas in other countries – anchor babies, so-called."

For seventeen months, they were held alongside serious criminals. A petition to free them was started by two Biloela social workers, Angela Fredericks and Brownwyn Dendle. They were the LNP-voting wives of local coalminers. The petition lit up the internet and airwaves. Alan Jones and Barnaby Joyce lobbied the government to release the Biloela family. "They're liked by the community, they're not on the dole, they're not on the crime pages," said Joyce. "Their kids were born in Australia. You may as well send them to Rwanda, because that's another country they weren't born in."

Courts upheld Dutton's judgement Nades and Priya were not legitimate asylum seekers. In August 2019, the family were forced onto a flight back to Sri Lanka. At the last minute, a legal injunction derailed the deportation. They were taken to Christmas Island Detention Centre. Dutton's stubbornness was contrasted with his sympathy towards white au pairs. Anthony Albanese was the new Opposition leader. He called for Dutton to "just do a cut and paste" from the au pair decisions. Dutton retorted that Albanese needed to stop trying to be "Mr Compassionate."

Dutton complained about the legal expenses. Meanwhile, it cost the Morrison government $30 million to reopen Christmas Island and staff it with guards. The only inmates in the prison in the middle of the Indian Ocean were the couple and their two children. In July 2020, Priya was rushed to Perth with complaints of abdominal pains and vomiting. "I wish her every good health and a speedy return back to Sri Lanka," said Dutton. "But this is … ridiculous. It is unfair on their children. And it sends a very bad message to other people who think they can rort the system as well."

In June 2021, three-year-old Tharnicaa was rushed to Perth. She was diagnosed with a blood infection caused by pneumonia. Her mother claimed it had been ignored by detention centre staff. The family was released into community detention, anxiously awaiting exile. In August 2022, under a Labor government, they were granted permanent residence.

Lifelong Liberal voters hounded inner-urban Liberal MPs about Dutton's inflexibility on the Biloela family. It added to the backlash against the Coalition's approach to climate change. So did the government's handling of Australia's #MeToo moment. Peter Dutton called the Brittany Higgins case "she said, he said." On Twitter, a refugee activist named Shane Bazzi accused Dutton of being "a rape apologist." For the former rape detective, it was beyond the pale. Dutton sued Bazzi for defamation.

The #MeToo moment also felled Linda Reynolds, the defence minister, who employed Brittany Higgins and Bruce Lehrmann. By now, professional female voters were abandoning the Liberals in droves. Albanese was uninspiring, albeit not despised like Shorten. In this new national mood, his soft touch was a strength. Morrison was regarded by moderates who voted for him as the most incompetent prime minister in recent history.

Dutton had every right to sit on his hands and say: "I told you so." But he was a bigger man than that. Desperate times called for desperate wedges. Dutton went beyond Howard, back to Menzies. He conjured up an old bogeyman that could give the Coalition an edge: reds under the bed.

*

In March 2021, Peter Dutton was appointed the Minister for Defence. He visited a military base in Townsville for a XXXX Gold with soldiers. They were under siege from revelations about the unlawful killing of civilians in Afghanistan. Dutton wanted to get their unfiltered opinions. He told the cameraman and senior officers to leave. "Dutts is at the helm," LNP MP Phil Thompson – an Afghanistan war veteran – told Sky News.

Dutton overturned a decision by the ADF chief, Angus Campbell, to strip awards from special forces troops who'd served in Afghanistan. Then Dutton banned Defence from hosting morning teas for the International Day Against Homophobia, Biphobia, Interphobia and Transphobia (IDAHOBIT). ADF staff had been encouraged to wear rainbow clothing and ally pins. "We are not pursuing a woke agenda," Dutton told Nine Newspapers.

Dutton was preparing the army for war, not a Mardi Gras parade. Australia was an "ally" to the United States. On ABC TV's *Insiders*, Dutton openly canvassed military conflict between China and Taiwan. America had been sharpening its rhetoric. So had the Chinese Communist Party. In September, Morrison added an unwoke acronym to the national lexicon: AUKUS. It was a military alliance with America and the United Kingdom, delivering a nuclear-powered submarine fleet to Australia. The projected cost would eventually balloon to between $268 billion and $368 billion. "Peace doesn't come for free," Dutton told the *Australian Financial Review*.

Morrison and Dutton desperately wanted a national security election. Anthony Albanese wasn't going to hand them a wedge. He offered automatic support for AUKUS. The main voice of dissent came from Paul Keating in a speech at the National Press Club. "Eight submarines against China when we get the submarines in twenty years' time – it'll be like throwing a handful of toothpicks at the mountain," he said. Keating stuck to his usual line and length. Australia needed to find security *in* Asia, not *from* Asia.

On Twitter, Dutton called his nemesis "Grand Appeaser Comrade Keating." The defence minister was profiled in *The Australian*. The headline: "Peter Dutton a hard man with the right stuff." The CCP had lifted 800 million people out of poverty. China's military budget was $252 billion, with 2.5 million soldiers. But the nuclear superpower had another thing coming for them: Dutts. "It would be inconceivable that we wouldn't support the US in an action if the US chose to take that action," said Dutton.

This was a significant shift in rhetoric. Dutton was speaking without the imprimatur of the National Security Committee. Penny Wong accused the government of embarking on "the most dangerous election strategy in Australian history." Dutton accused Wong of crumbling in "a fit of weakness," and of not defending Australian values against the Chinese. During Question Time in February 2022, he accused Albanese of being the CCP's handpicked candidate. Advance took Dutton's insinuation of treason and ran with it. Mobile billboards were driven around Australian cities. A grinning

Xi Jinping was superimposed over the Chinese flag, dropping a vote for Labor into a ballot box. "CCP SAYS VOTE LABOR," read the billboard.

In April 2021, China signed a security agreement with Solomon Islands. Xi Jinping was trying to encircle Australia by wooing its Pacific neighbours. The same nations Peter Dutton once joked about being wiped out by rising sea levels. "We don't bribe people," said Dutton, which was questionable given revelations still to come about the activities of Australian companies on Manus Island and Nauru. "The Chinese certainly do."

On Anzac Day 2022, Dutton attended a dawn service in Kallangur. Then he went to the Samford RSL. Dutton sent a stern warning to Xi Jinping via Karl Stefanovic on Nine's *Today Show*. "We have to be realistic that people like Hitler and others aren't just a figment of our imagination or that they're consigned to history," said Dutton. He cited the killing of innocent women and children in Ukraine as evidence.

"But how will you possibly stop it?" asked Stefanovic.

"Well, Karl, the only way that you can preserve peace is to prepare for war and to be strong as a country, not to cower, not to be on bended knee and be weak," said Dutton.

The results were mixed. Even Queensland farmers and coalminers knew that Australia relied on trade with China. Xenophobia wasn't dead. But was courting war with China an election winner? Communists had been replaced in the nightmares of voters by Islamic terrorists and boat people. In the minds of Quiet Australians, the CCP was no Al-Qaeda; Xi Jinping no Osama bin Laden.

The Coalition were perhaps a victim of their own success. Howard had presided over record-breaking migration from East Asia. Australians with Chinese ancestry represented 5.5 per cent of the country, or almost 1.4 million people. They paid close attention to the scare campaign. It was interpreted by many as the renaissance of Yellow Peril rhetoric. A former Liberal MP – who lost an electorate with a large population of Mandarin-speakers – estimates that six seats can be decided by the Chinese-Australian vote. "Morrison and Dutton took a baseball bat to our relationship with

Chinese Australians," says the defeated Liberal MP. "And they took a baseball bat to us."

At the 2022 election, in the ten seats with the highest proportion of Mandarin-speakers, the Liberals suffered an 8.46 per cent swing, compared to 5.47 per cent overall. The Liberals lost Reid, Bennelong and Chisholm. They very nearly lost Menzies in outer-suburban Melbourne, where 26.7 per cent of voters had Chinese ancestry. There, the Liberals suffered a swing of 6.34 per cent, winning the seat by 0.68 per cent.

There was a sensible middle ground available. Take Chinese expansionism seriously, and carefully seek to contain it through enhanced multilateral relations, without unnecessarily placing Australia in the crosshairs of a nuclear superpower. Malcolm Turnbull and Kevin Rudd both condemned the warmongering. Rudd saw it as emanating from "the Queensland Far-Right School of International Relations," more Joh Bjelke-Petersen than Malcolm Fraser. "Dutton represents the reverse of Theodore Roosevelt's dictum to 'speak softly and carry a big stick,'" wrote Rudd.

Dutton took the populist option. There was no length he wouldn't go to simulate strength. His bad cop persona followed him from welfare; to health; to immigration. There, he was shooting fish in a barrel. But China isn't a fish in a barrel, and diplomacy isn't a dick-measuring competition. The fight for peace won't be won by a tough guy with a loud mouth and a small stick.

Scott Morrison – a self-confessed "bulldozer" – shoulder-charged an eight-year-old soccer player in the final week of the 2022 election campaign. On D-Day, he proceeded to bulldoze the Liberal Party's remarkably durable broad church. The Coalition pandered to patriots, coalminers and Christians, while alienating professional women, West Australians and Chinese-Australian voters. Meanwhile, outer-suburban and regional Labor voters failed to be recruited by Morrison's dog whistles on trans athletes.

"This grand plan about flipping working-class Labor seats is a pipe-dream," a federal Liberal MP told me forty-eight hours before the election. "There are too many seats in the inner city we rely on to form government. People think Morrison is running some genius political operation. He's making shit up as he goes along."

Morrison's demolition job solidified power in the hands of the conservative faction who had antagonised the lost moral middle class. Tony Abbott absolved himself of blame for the disintegration of the base. He was happy for the Liberals to jettison a stable, monogamous relationship with the voters of Wentworth and co. for the fickle affection of some Western Sydney swingers. "Our voting heartland is shifting from places like Vaucluse to places like Penrith," he said. "There is a long-term trend for relatively affluent people to vote more to the left and relatively less affluent people to vote more to the right."

Abbott was speaking from experience. In 2019, he had lost Warringah to independent Zali Steggall. According to him, seats like Warringah were a lost cause. For his allies, this was a thrilling thesis. They didn't need to change. The voting landscape would change to accommodate them. And they could kiss goodbye the moderates who destroyed his prime ministership. "We saw it with Donald Trump's win in the US," said Abbott. "He basically won the flyover states. He didn't win the rich east coast and west coast."

Abbott is better at repeating three-syllable slogans than political science or basic geography. In 2019, 87 per cent of Australians lived within fifty kilometres of the coast. Australia doesn't have America's glut of heartland states filled with rust belts, nor the political system that makes them disproportionately powerful. Australia's geographical equivalent of the Midwest is the Northern Territory. The NT has a total of two lower-house and two upper-house seats. Roughly 60 per cent of Americans live in the South and the Midwest. By comparison, over 60 per cent of Australians live in Sydney, Melbourne, Brisbane, Perth and Adelaide. At the 2022 election, of the fifty-one federal electorates that cover Australia's two biggest cities, the Liberals won ten. Seven in Sydney and three in Melbourne. They won just two seats in Perth and one in Adelaide. They also lost two seats in Brisbane to the Greens. "We can get back into government with whoever is going to win back seats like Warringah," says Liberal MP Bridget Archer. "Which is not going to be Tony Abbott. I think we've established that."

The Liberal Party's slim pickings in Australia's main cities might present less of an existential crisis if they held a vice-like grip on seats beyond them. But they don't. Outside of Queensland, the Liberals didn't win a single seat in Australia's other biggest population bases: Canberra, Newcastle, the Central Coast, Wollongong, Hobart, Geelong, Darwin, Ballarat, Bendigo and Maitland. What the hell happened? Well, the canonisation of the "Howard battlers" happened. Beating up on inner-city elites worked superbly for the Liberals when federal elections were decided by a smattering of outer-suburban and regional marginal seats. Less so when its original target audience left en masse for candidates who weren't openly hostile to their existence. "The Liberal Party has lost its way," says Archer. "It has been infiltrated by beliefs that I don't think Menzies conceived it to represent."

The 2022 election represented the end of a 76-year duopoly for the major parties. In the lower house, 31.72 per cent of Australians voted for an option other than Labor or the Coalition. That figure compared to 14.53 per cent in 2007, 6.91 per cent in 1983 and 3.76 per cent in 1949. In the commentariat, conventional wisdom suggested the Liberal Party would adapt to the result by becoming more socially progressive. Conventional wisdom was wrong. Some wanted to replace the broad church with a chapel of culture warriors worshipping at the altar of John Howard. "The good thing about the last federal election is a lot of those lefties are gone," said Teena McQueen – then federal Liberal vice-president – at the 2022 CPAC Conference. "We need to renew with good conservative candidates."

In the federal Coalition, there was cross-party support for Abbott's thesis that the loss of inner-metropolitan seats was part of an inevitable global trend. At the same CPAC conference, LNP senator Matt Canavan expounded upon his view that the Coalition needed to embrace "boganisation." He declared that more working-class voters were up for grabs. "The left-of-centre parties around the world, including the Labor Party, have deserted non-tertiary educated people," said Canavan. "If we've got the guts to do it, we basically have the opportunity to have a permanent majority."

On *Sky After Dark*, Ray Hadley and Paul Murray rejoiced about the defeat of metropolitan moderates by the teals, while also raging at the six professional women who had just emasculated the Liberals. Murray dubbed them the "Tiffany independents." If Allegra Spender was so hot on climate change, asked Murray, why didn't she build a windmill in Centennial Park? "Of course, that would upset all of the dog walkers!" he said. "We mustn't allow that. Our staff need to be in peace. God bless the Tiffanys!"

Spender – the independent Wentworth MP – is a Cambridge-educated economist. Her grandfather was Sir Percy Spender, a Liberal MP for Warringah and cabinet minister in the Menzies government. Her father was John Spender, a Liberal MP for North Sydney. But in the echo chamber of Murray's man cave, Hadley is a better representation of Liberal values than Spender. Hadley also had an axe to grind with Matt Kean, the pro-renewables treasurer of the New South Wales Liberal government. "I'd say to Matt Kean tonight: either pee, or get off the pot," Hadley snarled. "One of the two. You're behaving like a teal with a green tinge. Wake up to yourself."

*

Matt Kean is a senior powerbroker in the moderate faction. He has Dutton's bald skull, but with bright eyes and a mischievous grin. "This is an existential crisis," he tells me at a café in Hornsby. "If we don't address the changing demographics of the country, the Liberal Party will become irrelevant."

Born in 1981, Kean is a millennial, the generation that has been deserting the Liberal Party in droves. His pessimism is backed up by post-election analysis from the Centre for Independent Studies, a Liberal-aligned think tank. The iron law of politics is that voters grow more conservative as they get older. According to the CIS, millennials are shifting to the Coalition at half the speed that boomers and gen X did. Gen Z are shifting *more* towards the left. By 2040, millennials and under will make up 70 per cent of the electorate. The CIS predicts the Coalition will lose another thirty-five seats if they don't arrest this generational drift. "Unless we are putting in place policies that will help young people enter the housing market, they are not going to touch us," says Kean. "But some people in the Liberal Party spend more time talking about which dunnys people use than tax reform."

Disillusionment with Australia's housing system is hitting critical mass. Over the next decade, this will be the defining issue of Australian politics. It transcends the climate and culture wars. Working-class families in the outer suburbs and regions are skipping meals to pay the rent, and sleeping in cars when they can't. University-educated millennials on six-figure salaries – so-called "inner-city elites" – have given up on the idea of buying their own home. "There is no future for conservative politics if more people, especially younger people, have nothing of their own to conserve," wrote conservative barrister Gray Connolly following the 2022 election.

Connolly is a self-identified Tory from Sydney's North Shore. He is far from a social progressive. Connolly's electorate is now held by a teal independent. He believes that the teal phenomenon had a lot to do with the lack of affordable housing. And he believes that Dave Sharma wouldn't have gained a single extra vote from renters in Wentworth if he rode a float at the Mardi Gras parade, because he reminded them of their landlords.

"Millennials are hitting thirty-five with no home and a shitload of student debt," Connolly tells me. "They are not going to vote Liberal. They see the Liberal Party as the people who ruined their lives."

The Liberal Party is suffering from a split personality. Peter Dutton has tunnel vision on battlers in the outer suburbs. Yet he remains committed to tax loopholes that disproportionately benefit the wealthy inner-city seats lost to the teals.

"Are we the party of inner-city anaesthetists who vote teal and own ten rentals?" asked Liberal MP Keith Wolahan, following the 2022 election. "Or are we the party of young families looking to own their first piece of Australia? Every lever must be on the table."

Wolahan is the first-term MP for Menzies, the seat named after the creator of the Liberal Party. He was born in Dublin and went to a public high school in outer-suburban Melbourne. His working-class dad studied at TAFE to become a roof plumber. For Wolahan, "aspirational" isn't just a vapid buzzword. Wolahan worries that Australia is becoming the kind of class-divided society his parents fled. "Hard work and intellect don't matter as much now," he tells me. "It's the randomness of whether your parents own land or not."

Wolahan wants an open debate about cutting tax loopholes for property investors. He believes that young people will punish political parties that don't address the housing crisis. Interestingly, he suggests that major tax reform in this area might need to be an inside job: led by the Liberal Party, rather than Labor. "Is the residential property market just another investment class?" asks Wolahan. "If you're answer to that is yes, I don't think that you're serious about solving this problem."

Wolahan is "live and let live" Liberal, but he is not a member of the moderate faction. He bemoans identity politics on the left and right. He was the first Liberal MP to publicly express regret for Robodebt. When we spoke over the phone in September 2023, he had just been to a funeral for a trans woman: Nerissa Marshall, an ex-priest and Liberal Party supporter. "If we adapt our values to the new Australia, I think we have got a bright future," Wolahan told me. "If we close our eyes and pretend like Australia hasn't changed and don't shift and be bloody-minded about it, I think we're at risk."

Wolahan isn't alone in the federal Liberal caucus. But some are less shy than others about breaking cover. In the current term of parliament, the only major-party politician to float changes to negative gearing has been a Liberal: Maria Kovacic. Kovacic ran for the outer-suburban seat of Parramatta at the 2022 election. She lost. In 2023, she secured a federal Senate vacancy for the Liberal Party. Her maiden speech broke a Liberal taboo. "We should not be afraid to consider tax changes," said Kovacic, "whether they be capping the number of properties that can be negatively geared [or] working with the states to replace stamp duty."

Kovacic was speaking from lived experience of precariousness. Her parents fled from war in the Balkans to Australian migrant camps. Then, as a young single mother to three children in Western Sydney, banks and welfare agencies ignored Kovacic's pleas for empathy. So did her landlord and the Family Court. "People weren't listening to a woman," she tells me. "People weren't listening to someone who didn't look or sound like them. If something went wrong in your life, you must be to blame."

Kovacic presents a ray of hope for the regeneration of a progressive streak within the federal Liberal Party. In an interview at the Parramatta Leagues Club, she cites Menzies and the pro-home ownership philosophy of the "Forgotten People" speech. Kovacic wants her party to place professional women and millennial renters at the heart of its electoral pitch. "I'm not okay with the fact that some young Australians have taken the view that they will never be able to afford their own home," she tells me. "And that someone over here can have half-a-dozen homes; or ten, or fifteen, or twenty … That's not right."

John Howard was offering battlers more than platitudes. Rightly or wrongly, many working-class and lower-middle-class voters *did* become asset-rich from Howard's property boom. Hence their electoral loyalty. The problem is they snatched the ladder up. The working class of the twenty-first century is more feminine and ethnically diverse. And they are much less socially mobile, thanks to the deterioration of the Australian dream.

*

RedBridge director Tony Barry grasps the contradictions in the Coalition like few others. After a Catholic education in coal-rich Central Queensland, he worked as a staffer for Christopher Pyne and Malcolm Turnbull. Barry was deputy state director of the Victorian Liberal Party during Howard's fruitful marginal seat campaign at the 2004 election. He is clear-eyed about the lack of ethnic and generational diversity within the Liberal base. "The Liberal membership is whiter than a Mormon golf tournament," he tells me. "They think *Sky After Dark* is representative of the real world."

Barry argues the party needs to modernise a policy platform geared towards expiring boomers. He can't see a path to government that doesn't include some of the seats lost to teals. He sees the structural weaknesses of the Liberal Party as being a bigger issue than Dutton himself, whom he has known since 2001. Barry repeats the same positive appraisals of Dutton's behind-the-scenes personality, though it is his intuitive understanding of marginal seats on the urban fringe that Barry sees as his great political strength. "Dutton comes from the outer suburbs," says Barry. "He gets them. Albanese is from Marrickville. He was built to communicate to the inner city."

Dutton is pursuing a Suburban Strategy. This is the down under franchise of the Republicans' Southern Strategy, when the traditional party of America's northeast elite snubbed New York to seduce the gun-loving south. "The whole secret of politics is knowing who hates who," said Kevin Phillips, a strategist for Nixon, the president who realigned US politics.

The Suburban Strategy – heedless as it seems to some – makes sense if the priority is finding a narrow path to power for Dutton. Not reconstituting the Liberal Party in the image of Malcolm Turnbull, protecting the job prospects of moderate Liberals and appeasing electorates that probably won't return to a party presided over by Dutton and his conservative faction.

A united right wing doesn't guarantee majority government, but it has the potential to be the largest slice of the electoral pie. As Labor looks like getting raided from the left by the defection of renters to the Greens, Dutton wants to carve off voters from the right.

Much like the voters it covets, the Liberal Party's lust for the outer suburbs is very much aspirational, though. Of the forty-two electorates classified as "outer metropolitan" by the Australian Electoral Commission, Labor holds twenty-five. Thirteen are held with two party–preferred margins larger than 10 per cent. The Coalition holds fourteen outer-metropolitan electorates. Just one of them – Mitchell – is held by the Liberals, with a margin larger than 10 per cent. At the 2022 election, Labor suffered massive swings in outer-suburban Melbourne seats. But most first preferences went to minor parties, before trickling back to Labor.

"Conservatives believe that there is a pot of gold waiting at the end of the rainbow in outer-suburban Sydney and Melbourne," says an ex-Liberal MP who lost to a teal. "It doesn't exist. I think it will take the poison pill of repeated election defeats to generate serious change."

There are forty-five inner-metropolitan seats. Dutton is happy to leave Labor, the Greens and the teals to squabble over them. He is concentrating on the ninety-six outer-suburban, provincial and rural electorates. This strategy makes great mathematical sense if you ignore the ethnic diversity of outer-suburban Sydney and Melbourne and the monoculturalism of the Coalition.

Dutton's political playbook translates fluently enough to outer-suburban and provincial seats in New South Wales and Victoria that have similar demographics to Dickson, where 76.8 per cent of residents were born in Australia. Such as Lindsay, where the figure is 71.5 per cent. But he has little experience speaking to electorates in Sydney and Melbourne with significant Asian and Middle Eastern diasporas. "This is where Dutton's suburban strategy comes unstuck," says a senior Labor minister. "There aren't enough seats like Lindsay in Western Sydney."

Dutton wants to make outer-suburban and regional voters down south see they have more in common with the voters of Queensland than the "elites" running their own capital cities. It would take a history-making realignment, no less seismic in nature than Menzies' recruitment of Catholics, Whitlam's recruitment of graduates and Howard's recruitment of blue-collar battlers. Is Dutton leading the Liberal Party into an electoral cul-de-sac? Or does he know something about Australia that the political class is missing?

Dutton must understand – in his heart of hearts – that winning back eighteen seats in one term will take a miracle. But he doesn't need a miracle in 2025. From the wellspring of Morrison's history-making unpopularity, Labor got a fragile majority. It is extremely conceivable a slew of seats will correct to the Liberals next time, especially in Western Australia.

A modest three-seat increase for Dutton would plunge Albanese into minority government. Assuming Dutton is conducting a two-term strategy, he'd rather get the teal seats back at the second election, to spare the perilous implications for his leadership of an influx of urban moderates. Abbott's realignment would be less of a pipedream against a Labor Party in minority government with the Greens. A ten-seat gain would place Dutton within striking distance of forming minority government. "If you're in a minority situation, of course you would negotiate like buggery to pull a government together," Dutton told Nine Newspapers in 2022.

It is a surprisingly honest admission by an Opposition leader, and a tacit acknowledgement that minority governments might be the way of the near future. Dutton knows that the current crossbench aren't all total lefties. Dai Le and Rebekha Sharkie are ex-Liberals. Allegra Spender and Kate Chaney belong to prominent Liberal families. Helen Haines holds a seat that had been conservative for eight decades. Bob Katter is an ex-National. But Katter, their most kindred spirit, doesn't think much of the Opposition.

"I don't want to speak derogatorily," Katter tells me. "But the Liberal Party are just completely bereft of talent. Dutton is not bereft of talent. But he's got no one else. The other side have got a lot of formidable people."

Dutton is on a one-man mission to destroy a government.

Peter Dutton's political career was leading towards the Voice referendum. It was a fight about enshrining within the constitution an advisory body representing Aboriginal and Torres Strait Islander Australians. The case was prosecuted by lawyers and academics, with the endorsement of elders after an exhaustive series of regional dialogues.

"Proportionally, we are the most incarcerated people on the planet," read the Uluru Statement from the Heart. "We are not an innately criminal people. Our children are aliened from their families at unprecedented rates."

On election night in 2022, Anthony Albanese committed to the Uluru Statement from the Heart "in full." The creation of an advisory body would be followed by a truth-telling and national treaty process. No referendum had passed without bipartisan support from the major parties. Now, the Liberals were led by a man who boycotted the Apology. How on earth could he say yes?

For a while, Dutton seems to be hedging his bets and pulling his punches. Polls consistently show support for the Voice registering over 65 per cent. The Yes vote is expected to be especially strong within the highly educated teal electorates that had abandoned the Liberal Party at the 2022 election.

Dutton appoints Julian Leeser – a loyal proponent of the Voice – as the Coalition's shadow minister for Indigenous affairs. Even if the Liberals don't officially support the Yes campaign, they might run dead on the issue.

In October 2022, Dutton pays a visit to Alice Springs. The new National Party senator for the Northern Territory is Jacinta Nampijinpa Price. She is a 41-year-old Aboriginal mother of four, and a survivor of domestic violence. In her maiden speech, Price railed against Welcomes to Country, the removal of grog bans and cashless welfare cards from Alice Springs, and the Uluru Statement from the Heart. "My goal is to halt the pointless virtue-signalling," she said. Price blamed "left-wing elites" for ignoring the scourge of "black-on-black violence" and poisoning the relationship between police and Aboriginal children. She is beloved by the right-wing establishment for her political incorrectness. Mining billionaire Gina Rinehart was watching from the gallery.

On Dutton's visit to Alice Springs, Price provides a tour of the locations where family members have died of murder, suicide and alcohol abuse. She is worried that Dutton might capitulate to the metropolitan moderates on the Voice. "As much as it was frustrating at times, having got to know Peter, I knew that he would get there, he had a plan," she said later.

Dutton has been bruised by his denial of the Apology to the Stolen Generations. Whatever his personal inclinations, there is probably no way that he can support the Voice without the Coalition eating itself alive. Publicly, he needs to keep an open mind, until the point Labor tips his hand.

In late October 2022, Pauline Hanson releases a statement titled: "Will the real Peter Dutton please stand up?" "The man I once admired for his values and his strong, dogged approach is withering on the vine," says Senator Hanson. "I thought Peter Dutton might have been a brilliant prime minister but for more than 150 days since he took the top job as Opposition leader, Australians have hardly heard boo from him." She calls the appointment of Leeser "pathetic." Her dream replacement? Jacinta Price.

"Grow a set, Peter," says Pauline.

At the end of November, National Party leader David Littleproud declares his party will formally oppose the Voice. He is heavily influenced by the pro-No position of Price. She calls the referendum "emotional blackmail" by elites, comparing the effect to "coercive control." Noel Pearson fiercely condemns Price as the new Pauline Hanson. "It's a tragic redneck celebrity vortex that she's caught up in and it involves right-wing [think tanks]," says Pearson. "They're the string-pullers … And their strategy was to find a Blackfella to punch down on other Blackfellas." This is a taste of what is coming for Dutton if he decides to oppose the Voice. He can't just say no. He needs to cultivate an alternative moral high ground to occupy.

*

On 10 January 2023, George Pell dies. In 2020, the former Catholic archbishop and cardinal had been acquitted of sexually molesting young boys by the High Court. Pell's reputation remained tainted by the Royal Commission into Institutional Responses to Child Sexual Abuse. At the very least, he failed to adequately address conspicuous evidence of paedophilia.

"On his passing, the fact [Pell] spent a year in prison for a conviction that the High Court of Australia unanimously quashed should provide some cause for reflection for the Victorian Labor government and its institutions that led this modern-day political persecution," says Dutton.

During the mourning period for Pell, Dutton's attention turns to paedophilia further afield. The crime crisis in Alice Springs grips the national media. Dutton calls for the immediate reinstatement of "grog bans" and the deployment of the AFP to tame delinquents and save children. "It breaks my heart … and it's an unsavoury subject to talk about," says Dutton, "but the fact is that the prevalence of child sexual abuse in these communities will condemn – particularly young girls – to a lifetime of difficulty."

Dutton claims that Australians wouldn't tolerate such human depravity in the woke bubbles of inner-city Sydney, Melbourne, Brisbane and Canberra. Just over a week later, Dutton meets with the Referendum Working Group for the Voice via video link. This is so that he can attend the funeral for Pell. It is held at St Mary's Cathedral near the Sydney CBD. Dutton is joined at the funeral by John Howard, Tony Abbott, Mark Latham and Alan Jones. Pell's protégé, Abbott, gives a eulogy. He calls the criminal proceedings against Pell "a modern form of crucifixion."

It takes a lot for Ray Hadley to disagree with Dutton. In a monologue before their weekly radio chat, Hadley condemns Pell for "turning a blind eye" to paedophilia. Dutton comes on the line. Hadley tries to change the subject. But Dutton has something to get off his chest. He praises the Catholic Church for confessing to "the mistakes of the past." Australians regularly acknowledge Indigenous culture, he says. But they also shouldn't forget the contribution of the churches. Nor should they rush to judge Pell based upon left-wing hatchet jobs. "You're innocent until you're proven guilty, and a court makes a finding or a jury makes a finding of guilt or innocence," says Dutton. "We're not convicting people in our country on the vibe."

Attention shifts to common ground. The Reserve Bank has decided to replace King Charles on the $5 note with an Indigenous design. Dutton slams this as "woke nonsense," unsupported by "the silent majority." He warns that Australia Day, the national anthem and the flag are next on the chopping block. And he calls for Albanese to stage an urgent intervention in Alice Springs. "Tragically, somebody's going to be killed," says Dutton. "If you've got kids running around with machetes and axes, it's inevitable."

Dutton remains coy about his position on the Voice. But he is tilling the soil for a different debate. He wants to anchor that conversation in the present. To focus on the break-ins and rapes happening now, rather than the massacres and kidnappings in the past. He absolves Australians of ongoing guilt for the Stolen Generations. Indeed, he appears to be advocating for a less blatantly racist child removal program. "Because we're talking about Indigenous kids, you can't take them away from their family, put them into a safe environment where they can sleep at night without being annoyed by adults or molested by somebody," says Dutton.

This is news to the Stolen Generations survivors who were taken from their families and then sexually abused at boys and girls homes run by Christians. The history wars continue. Way back in 1862, Dutton's great-great-grandfather, Charles, had pinpointed the double standard in the media coverage of Australian race relations. "The public but rarely, if ever, hear of the cruelties, goading to madness, which the blacks suffer at the hands of the native police," he wrote to *The Sydney Morning Herald*. "On the contrary, any act of violence by the blacks is quickly known throughout the colonies, and without any inquiry into the treatment that may have caused it, a universal cry of execration and hatred follows."

Charles Dutton wanted to broker peace. In *Seven Versions of an Australian Badland*, Ross Gibson wrote that Charles Dutton and his brother Henry were "hoping for an easier style of hegemony, something self-sustaining where the various classes felt the system of power to be procedural and inevitable rather than forcibly and endlessly asserted." This sounds remarkably similar to what the Voice was aiming to facilitate: a partnership from the grassroots up, rather than a top-down police state. It is difficult not to conclude that Peter Dutton's nineteenth-century squatter kin had a more forward-thinking approach to reconciliation than he does.

*

In March 2023, Anthony Albanese announces the proposed question for the referendum, and the proposed amendment to the constitution. Hubristically, he no longer believes the Voice needs bipartisan support to succeed. Shortly afterwards, a byelection is held in Aston. It is an outer-metropolitan seat in Melbourne's eastern mortgage belt. Not too rich. Not too poor. This has been Dutton's target audience since entering politics. A sitting government hasn't taken a seat from the Opposition at a byelection since 1920.

Labor runs a negative campaign, trumpeting Dutton's inflammatory language about China to the 14.1 per cent of Aston with Chinese ancestry. Labor wins Aston for the first time since 1987. It is interpreted by many in the media as a potential death knell for Dutton's leadership. According to moderate Liberals and pragmatic conservatives, the party needs to abandon the ongoing obsession with stoking culture war issues to focus on their traditional political strengths: economics and the cost of living. Dutton goes on *Insiders* the Sunday morning after the Aston byelection result. "The [trans] debate runs two ways," Dutton tells host David Speers. "There are very strong views within many parts of Australian society. Maybe not here within the inner-city areas of the country. But within the outer-metropolitan areas, this is an issue … that has parents and others very worked up."

A Newspoll is released that night. Labor leads the Coalition 55–45 on a two-party preferred basis. Albanese's net satisfaction rating is +22. Dutton's is −13. When forced to choose between Yes and No in the forthcoming referendum, 58 per cent of respondents are in favour.

To Dutton's thinking, there is nothing wrong with the Suburban Strategy. His Forgotten People just haven't heard him clearly enough yet. He goes double-or-nothing. Four days after the Aston byelection, Dutton announces that the Liberal Party will formally oppose the Voice. And that he will be actively campaigning for Australians to reject it. There will be no conscience vote, due to the overwhelming mood of the party room. "There was a resounding No to the Prime Minister's Canberra Voice," he says, citing the lack of detail provided by the government as a justification.

Dutton frames the Voice as a personal thought bubble of Albanese. It is textbook Tony Abbott, who coined the phrase "Keating's Republic" when he was the head of the monarchist movement. This flies in the face of the facts, but it is incredibly effective. For many disengaged voters, the Voice becomes the first big proposal they associate with Albanese.

The idea for the Voice had originated under a Liberal government and was supported by Ken Wyatt, the then Liberal minister for Indigenous affairs. According to Wyatt, Dutton never once questioned him about the rationale for the Voice when they were in cabinet together. Now, Wyatt quits the Liberal Party in disgust. Later, he accuses Dutton of copying the "fake news" tactics of Trump. The only serving MP who picks up the phone to Wyatt is Julian Leeser. Leeser subsequently resigns from the shadow ministry. "Our future is not in American glitz, and Trumpian red hats, or a political diet of anger," he says in a speech during the referendum campaign.

Suddenly, Dutton has a vacancy on his shadow front bench. He takes off to Alice Springs for a FIFO visit with Jacinta Price. Dutton seeks expertise from shoppers and small businesspeople. He is rebuked for not meeting with the Lhere Artepe Aboriginal Corporation. At a press conference, he accuses such groups of turning a blind eye to the sexual abuse of children. An ABC journalist asks what evidence he is relying on.

"That's such an ABC question," says Dutton. "Do you live locally?"

"I live locally," says the journalist.

Dutton is indignant. He has spoken to cops and social workers. He paints a vivid picture of a screaming six-year-old, begging to be saved from abuse. The NT police minister, Kate Worden, calls this "a dog act." She blasts Dutton for showing little interest in Alice Springs until now. Worden also points out that it is mandatory in the Northern Territory to report claims of child abuse. "You cannot keep throwing our children out as if they are all being abused, as though everyone is a paedophile, when there is no evidence to back it up," says Arrernte and Luritja woman Catherine Liddell, the CEO of SNAICC. "They are not fodder for media. They are not fodder for politicians." Eventually, Dutton clarifies that he hasn't raised any specific complaints of sexual abuse. He was going off the vibe.

*

The following week, Pauline Hanson's dream comes true: Dutton announces the appointment of Jacinta Price as the shadow minister for Indigenous Australians. The trips to Alice Springs had been a set-piece for this. In an effort to destroy Albanese, and save himself, Dutton reinvents himself as a passionate defender of legal tradition. "You can't out-legislate the constitution," says Dutton, flanked by Price.

That is the crux of Dutton's public opposition. He doesn't necessarily disagree with the establishment of the Voice, or with constitutional recognition for First Nations people. He is suddenly in love with the idea of *symbolic* recognition, now that it is the lesser of two threats to raw authority. But to enshrine the Voice in the constitution is a recipe for mayhem.

Advance is crop-dusting the continent with misinformation about the Voice. The group has a laser-like focus on the outer suburbs of Brisbane, Adelaide and Perth. Price becomes the face of their resistance. An abstract legal critique is not going to flip low-information voters. Advance reframes the referendum as a debate about race. Hence: "The Voice of Division." Communications director Steve Doyle later explained the rationale. "We were convinced that forty-year-old females with two kids were not coming home from their part-time job … and looking up information about whether or not the voice was legally risky," Doyle told *The Australian*.

Volunteers for Advance makes hundreds of thousands of phone calls to persuadable voters. The call teams are instructed not to identify themselves as part of the official No campaign. Instead, they should good-naturedly sow "fear and doubt" by relying on emotion, not reason, nor incomprehensible legal jargon. "I've also heard that some of the people who helped design the Voice proposal are campaigning to abolish Australia Day," reads the script, "and want to use the Voice to push for compensation and reparations through a treaty."

Dutton adopts their framing. He calls the Voice an "Orwellian" attempt to demote white and migrant Australians to second-class citizens. Albanese hands Dutton an alibi for a prolonged debate about Indigenous Australians that he had carefully avoided since getting elected to parliament. Now Dutton pushes buttons for resentments that have been bubbling under the surface. "The Voice as proposed by the prime minister promotes difference," Dutton tells parliament at the end of May. "The Voice will re-racialise our nation."

In June 2023, Australia's mortgage belts undergo their fourth interest rate rise of the year. Roughly 600,000 households begin their segue from fixed-rate home loans to ones with variable rates. Disposable incomes evaporate. "Australians are saying: 'Sure, I want a better outcome for Indigenous Australians, but why won't the PM explain it to me?'" says Dutton. "And: 'Why is the PM yelling at me that I'm not smart enough to understand it, or that I'm racist because I don't support the Voice?'"

Dutton is conducting a four-step demolition job on the Voice. The first step is to derail a feel-good debate about the legal empowerment of Indigenous people with allegations of sexual abuse. The second step is to paint an advisory body as a nefarious power grab by black activists. The third is to frame Albanese as a patsy for corporate elites in Sydney and Melbourne, who funnel money to the Yes campaign while gutting the bank accounts of suburban mums and dads. The fourth is to present the Coalition as lone defenders of those economically distressed Forgotten People.

"I one hundred per cent believe that Dutton opposed the Voice for purely political reasons," Liberal MP Bridget Archer tells me. "It's straight out of the Tony Abbott playbook of just oppose everything."

Through winter, support for the Voice continues to decline. Conspiracy theories circulate about the neutrality of the Australian Electoral Commission.

At the referendum, voters will be asked to write "Yes" or "No" in a black box on the ballot. Ticks will count as Yeses. But crosses won't count as Noes. It is the continuation of tradition. No campaigners claim a conspiracy. Dutton endorses their paranoia. "I don't think we should have a process that's rigged," Dutton tells Ray Hadley, "and that's what the prime minister's tried to orchestrate from day one."

The prime minister announces that the referendum will take place on 14 October. Dutton calls for Albanese to cut his losses. Instead, Labor should legislate the Voice, and hold the referendum on constitutional recognition of Indigenous people. Dutton insists that he is sincerely committed to constitutional recognition. "I think it's right and respectful to recognise Indigenous Australians in the constitution," he says, promising another referendum if he becomes prime minister.

In August, Dutton makes a controversial appearance on ABC's *Kitchen Cabinet*. He takes Annabel Crabb on a tour of his farm; spruiks the benefits of meditation; and cooks her a potato-based seafood chowder. And he speaks about suffering flashbacks to cases as a cop. "I was a nineteen-year-old when I started policing. I had a fairly sheltered life in retrospect. And I just hadn't been exposed to that side. The viciousness of some people. The depravity of others. It's a small element of society, thank goodness. But it does stay with you. Because it jars. And I think it scars as well."

Crabb is criticised for humanising a divisive public figure. But she elicits unprecedented insight into Dutton's black-and-white psyche. It is impossible for him not to see Aboriginal people through the prism of law and order. "What is the thing that blows you away most about Indigenous culture in this country?" asks Crabb. Dutton launches into a lament about the lawlessness and "absolute squalor" of Alice Springs. Crabb suggests that he has missed the point of the question. Dutton argues that Aboriginal art and dance can be a smokescreen for an underbelly of violence.

This explains his default solution to the vast chasm between the health and economic outcomes of black and white Australians. A giant rape investigation. An endless intervention. Most Aboriginal Australians live in the cities and regions. Dutton has little to offer those in the inner city; those in the suburbs; those who aren't personal victims of horrific violence in the outback. Those who want the truth spoken, so that the wound of losing their country can heal. Dutton wants them to get over it. The Opposition leader regularly expects the country to confront and affirm his disturbing memories and premonitions. But he is the only one allowed to live in the past.

Malcolm Turnbull's office scrapes the sky of the Sydney CBD. Views of the harbour shimmer through the windows. He is thin and elegantly dressed, with a mellifluous voice that could cure a migraine. Is Turnbull the last liberal leader of the Liberals? It certainly seems that way. The ex–prime minister offers a condensed history of Menzies' Forgotten People and what happened to them. He blames the loss of nine traditional Liberal seats on the narrow pursuit of socially conservative voters in the outer suburbs and regions, with overblown rhetoric about issues such as boat people. And he partly blames their xenophobia on Murdoch's "right-wing angertainment ecosystem."

"It's essentially like a self-licking ice cream," says Turnbull. "You've got a section of the community fed a diet of anger, division and resentment. They are typically older, whiter people who have become a minority."

Turnbull confesses that centre-right parties use culture wars to wedge working-class voters from their economic self-interest. He provides a masterclass on why the one-eyed Liberals who flooded into the party room post-Howard found him so pompous and disloyal. He jokes that most of those faux conservatives wouldn't know Edmund Burke from Tony Burke. Rather than try to define the ideology of the Monkey Pod, he offers a witty jibe: "I remember I once asked Gough Whitlam about [Labor MP] Arthur Gietzelt's ideology. He said: 'Comrade, Arthur couldn't spell ideology.'"

Turnbull is in a bipartisan mood. He recently manned the hustings with Tanya Plibersek to campaign for the Voice. As prime minister, he framed the Voice as a "third chamber to parliament" and predicted that a referendum on the matter would "go down in flames." This was based on his bitter experience as the leader of Australia's republic movement. "Why would you listen to Malcolm Turnbull on referendums?" he asks now. "They're all geniuses. Let's hope they are. And I'm proved terribly wrong."

Turnbull has backflipped on his previous opposition to a constitutionally enshrined advisory body. He is going to vote Yes. But he insists that No will win, due to a country with a phobia for constitutional change. And he believes this would have been the result anyway, with or without Dutton's scare campaign. Turnbull's stately face flashes with a sympathy for Albanese, tinged with dread that Dutton is back from the dead.

"If it goes down, a lot of people will round on Albanese and say it's all his fault," says Turnbull. "He'll get blamed for something that was probably never winnable. And Dutton will seek to hang it around his neck."

Has Dutton been flogging a dead horse for no tangible gain? This is a fascinating thesis, shared privately by some moderate Liberal MPs. They fear that their leader has been overestimating his effect on the nosediving polls and interpreting them as vindication for Abbott's Suburban Strategy. It is possible that the suburbs will have forgotten all about the Voice by the next election, as inflation and interest rates fall. But the metropolitan small-l liberals will never forget the wrecking ball Dutton aimed at reconciliation.

*

Dutton is paying a visit to the seat of Lindsay. Opie Manufacturing Group are a fourth-generation family business, specialising in high-tech metalwork. Their factory is in Emu Plains, west of Penrith. This is Abbott's preferred heartland for the modern Liberal Party. There are less than four weeks until the referendum. Dutton is unflustered by Olympian Cathy Freeman's support of the Voice. Her grandmother was a member of the Stolen Generations. "I have the utmost respect for Cathy Freeman," says Dutton, "but there are lots of celebrities who are giving their support to the Yes vote. I think the average mums and dads out in the suburbs are the ones who are voting No."

The next day, Dutton is on a street walk through Mosman with Liberal MP Anne Ruston. They are visiting Abbott's old seat of Warringah. Dutton is on cloud nine. Josh Frydenberg has just announced he won't be standing at the next election. The most obvious roadblock to Dutton's two-term strategy is gone. There is a spring in his step and a gleam in his eye. If anything, he waxes *more* lyrical about the outer suburbs while on the Lower North Shore. "I'm talking about people in the suburbs," says Dutton. "Not inner-city elites – they'll vote for the Greens and they'll vote for the Voice."

The only way Dutton could make it plainer that he doesn't give a toss about the teal seats is if he burnt an effigy of Malcolm Turnbull on Bondi Beach. He condemns the intellectual snobbery of Albanese, Alan Joyce and the elites funding the Yes campaign. According to Dutton, Albanese and Joyce practically co-authored the Uluru Statement from the Heart. "They say, 'Look, if you just read slowly and maybe if you read the document twice, you'll be as smart as us and you'll understand it and you'll vote Yes.' Well, I think Australians are much smarter than the prime minister realises."

At some point, the pursuit of constitutional recognition for Indigenous Australians morphed into a referendum on whether or not people without university degrees deserve to be looked down upon as dumbarses by the highly educated. On and on and on it goes: Dutton plays Whac-A-Mole against academics, lawyers, CEOs, bankers and celebrities, at a time of great disgruntlement on Struggle Street. Meanwhile, Albanese attends a Yes23 rally in Marrickville. Ray Martin is the guest of honour. He manifests Dutton's caricature of Yes campaigners. "If you don't know, find out what you don't know," Martin tells the crowd. "What that slogan is saying is if you're a dinosaur or a dickhead … who can't be bothered reading, vote No."

Dutton demands an apology from Martin, but he is licking his lips. Trump had his deplorables. Now Dutton has his dinosaurs and dickheads.

*

The Opposition leader flies to Western Australia. He can smell an electoral correction in the air. The political hypnotist Mark McGowan is finally gone. Dutton pays a visit to a coffee shop in West Perth with Jacinta Price, the woman of the hour. Epic Espresso is owned by Vietnamese migrants – Hung and Tammy Luong – and run by son Albert. They are at financial breaking point. Price is a captivating retail politician: comfortable in her own skin and quick with a cheeky grin. Some compare her to Hanson. But there is none of Hanson's naked rage on her face. To the disengaged, her message is uplifting. "It doesn't matter whether we were here 60,000 years ago or six months ago: you are Australian, and it doesn't matter your racial heritage," says Price.

Price stands at the espresso machine frothing some milk. She brings the common touch Dutton lacks. She says the things that would get him in deep shit. Such as claiming that colonisation has no ongoing negative effect on Aboriginal Australians. Or calling for an audit of all Indigenous spending by the government. Once uttered by Price, the muzzle can come off Dutton and others. "She's not interested, you know, capital-city talks and, you know, academics sort of pontificating over how money can be spent," says Dutton. Price doesn't want your money, or your backyard, or to demean your Australian dream. She wants to forgive and forget. This is a tantalising olive branch to the Australians who are sick of the history lessons.

The next day, Dutton drives two hours south to Bunbury. He does a tour of Piacentini & Son, an earthmoving company started by an Italian migrant named Albert Piacentini. It now employs over a thousand people. Dutton accuses the prime minister of being seduced by "the top end of town" and forgetting about Labor's historical base: "the workers." "They can't afford to pay their bills under this Labor government," he says, "and you've got the prime minister off on this frolic in relation to the Voice."

"This frolic" distils the way Dutton sees most of the social justice issues that animate Labor's inner-city base. He paints Albanese as a scatter-brained dabbler, running an "experiment" with the money of taxpayers. According to Dutton, the PM is bored by the struggles of ordinary people. He isn't. His message is repetitive and philosophically inconsistent. But he has no qualms hammering home those stale soundbites day in, day out until the election. The single biggest electoral risk for Labor is swinging voters getting the impression that the PM has bigger fish to fry than the cost of living.

Dutton knows the Voice referendum is going down. In the process, he wants to illuminate the divide between the metropolitan knowledge class and everyone else. Dutton – in his mind – isn't playing to the fringes. He views himself as the mainstream. And he sees Wentworth and Marrickville as the fringe, not the centre, no more representative of middle Australia than western Queensland. On his last pitstop in Perth, he makes a speech to the Pastoralists & Graziers Association of WA, the R.M. Williams–wearing Bunyip Aristocracy. "The prime minister has been captured by elites," says Dutton.

Then Dutton flies to Braddon, a historically marginal seat on the west coast of Tasmania. This is the most economically depressed electorate in Australia. It is Monday on the final week of the referendum campaign. "If you're living in an outer-suburban area, the new Labor Party is not for you," he says, "it's for inner-city trendies and supporters of the Green movement. The Liberal Party – the Coalition – is today's party for the worker."

Many commentators have framed the Voice referendum as Australia's "Brexit moment." That was a battle between a nationalist majority and a cosmopolitan minority. If Dutton gets his way, the next election will be Australia's actual Brexit moment. He has exploited the referendum as a branding exercise for the realignment of Australian politics.

*

The referendum is a bloodbath: 60.1 per cent of Australian adults vote No. TV presenters declare the result before dinnertime. Dutton's home state of Queensland leads the pack with a No vote of 68.2 per cent. But Queensland alone can't be blamed for destroying the Voice. South Australia isn't far behind with 64.2 per cent No; Western Australia is 63.3; New South Wales is 59 per cent; Tasmania is 58.9; and Victoria is 54.2 per cent No.

"Dutton has cemented race hate into the body politic in a way we did not foresee last year but that now is very clear," writes Marcia Langton that morning in *The Saturday Paper*. "He has killed any hope of reconciliation."

The faultlines are roughly the same as in the 1999 republic referendum. Inner-city seats with a high proportion of university graduates vote Yes. Everywhere else votes No, with a few exceptions. According to a study by the ANU, 59.5 per cent of Australians with a postgraduate degree and 54.6 per cent of those with a bachelor's degree vote Yes. Conversely, 45 per cent of those who completed Year 12, 34.4 per cent with a TAFE certificate and 19.9 per cent who did not complete Year 12 vote Yes.

Just twenty of Labor's seventy-eight seats achieve a majority of Yes voters. The split in the electoral coalition of the ALP is plain for all to see. In Anthony Albanese's inner-city electorate of Grayndler, 49.3 per cent of residents have a university degree. The median weekly household income is $2388. The Yes vote is 74.64 per cent. In Adelaide's outer-metropolitan electorate of Spence, 9.5 per cent of residents have a university degree. The median weekly household income is $1278. The Yes vote is 27.8 per cent.

"The Voice referendum wasn't a division between black and white," says Barnaby Joyce. "It was a division between rich Australia and not-so-rich Australia. It showed a new divide … It showed the teal seats are beyond reach now. There's a new type of politics in Australia and it's a little bit Trumpian."

Australia's budget Donald Trump spends referendum night in Brisbane. At a press conference, Dutton tries to strike a statesmanlike pose. Jacinta Price holds back a smile. An Australian flag hangs over Dutton's right shoulder. He pays tribute to the campaign run by Advance. He calls for a ceasefire on the bitter divisions caused by Albanese's "divisive" referendum. He extends the hand of friendship to Indigenous Yes voters. Then he calls for a royal commission into sexual abuse in Indigenous communities and an audit of spending on Indigenous programs.

"You were part of a government that was in power for almost ten years, up until recently," says a journalist. "Why do you need to ask where that money was spent, as your government was spending it?"

This is a considerable difference to Trump in 2016. Dutton comes from the swamp. The crisis of poverty and crime in Alice Springs didn't begin in 2022. As Home Affairs minister, Dutton was personally responsible for law enforcement. In response to the question, Dutton's head bobbles.

"Australians are really doing it tough," he says.

Dutton and Price attend a private victory party at the Hyatt Regency Hotel. Gina Rinehart slips inside without taking questions. That night, Alice Springs locals go to a free gig by Paul Kelly at Anzac Oval. "If not now, then when?" he sings. "If not us, then who?" The mood is sombre but not shocked.

The following afternoon, a smaller crowd returns to Anzac Oval. They are celebrating the fiftieth anniversary of Congress, a health organisation for Aboriginals in Central Australia. The timing couldn't be worse. Bushfire smoke explodes from the horizon. The tone of the speakers is closer to eulogy. "Hope is no good for my heart," says Nancy, an Aboriginal grandmother who doesn't think she will live to see constitutional recognition of her people.

Vincent Forrester is a decorated Aboriginal activist. A grey ponytail and funereal blue eyes. He wears black jeans and boots. His sleeves are rolled up to reveal tattoos on both forearms. There is a packet of tobacco tucked in his top pocket. He rolls one and frowns. "My country doesn't love me," he says. "Dutton is just playing politics with the misery of Aboriginal people."

Forrester was one of the founders of the National Aboriginal Council. In the 1980s, he served as an adviser to Malcolm Fraser and Bob Hawke. He regrets giving Fraser so much grief during treaty negotiations. "I'm telling ya: even the Labor Party was more conservative than Fraser!" Forrester tells me. "What the fuck happened to the liberals in the Liberal Party?"

Howard happened to the Liberal Party. Dutton makes him keep happening. But Howard beat Paul Keating twenty-six years ago. Which was thirty years since Robert Menzies retired as the prime minister. Between 1966 and 1996, the Liberal Party changed dramatically. This wasn't prevented by Howard's adoration of Menzies. He knew that the greatest form of flattery was rejuvenation, not mimicry. Between 1996 and 2024, the Liberal Party has barely changed a bit. Dutton is stuck. So is the country.

On Monday, Dutton lets the cat out of the bag. The Liberal Party will officially not be rushing to hold a second referendum on the constitutional recognition of Aboriginal and Torres Strait Islander Australians. "I think it's clear that the Australian public is probably over the referendum process for some time," he says.

That week, Dutton goes for a victory lap at the Queensland LNP's State Council Meeting. The shindig is held at Eatons Hill Hotel, in the sprawl on Brisbane's northside. Up the guts of Dutton Country. Eatons Hill Hotel has hosted Vanilla Ice, Shaggy and Lil Jon. Dutton is the most pessimistic headliner since Marilyn Manson graced the stage. The dark wizard of wedge politics is daydreaming about the Forgotten People. They aren't middle-class. Nor necessarily Liberal voters. Not yet, anyway.

Dutton talks about power bills. He talks about petrol prices. He riffs about the existential distance between Marrickville and Kallangur. According to Dutton, four in ten Labor voters sided with the No campaign. He insists they aren't racist. He insists they aren't dumb, just because they live outside the inner-city. Dutton is welcoming these "dinosaurs and dickheads" with open arms. "They're working-class Australians," he says. "Many of them voted for the Labor Party at the last election. But they're not going to vote for the Labor Party at the next election. Because the Labor Party has left them."

Ian Leavers is the president of the Queensland Police Union. The same poker face as Dutton, but with a thinner skull and wingnut ears. In an op-ed for *The Courier Mail*, he provides an insight into the mindset of Queensland cops. Leavers calls the Voice "wasteful, self-flagellating, woke nonsense," supported by wealthy inner-city elites seeking to blame the sins of Aboriginal criminals on colonisation. He claims that the truth-telling and treaty process would be even less popular with Queenslanders than the Voice. "All police I have spoken to are very worried that the 'inner-city latte sippers' have grabbed control of the law-and-order agenda," writes Leavers, "and now wish to further attack police and water down laws … They are effectively offering a free pass to every rapist, domestic violence abuser, habitual home invader and car thief who tells police they identify as Aboriginal."

Queensland premier Annastacia Palasczuk appoints Leavers to a victims-of-crime advisory body. In Queensland, the LNP withdraws bipartisan support for the process of truth-telling and treaty. LNP state Opposition leader David Crusifalli cites Queensland's high No vote as justification. Palasczuk crabwalks away from her own platform. She argues that such proposals are doomed without bipartisan support.

"We need politicians to grow up … and they should not be elected until they know the true history of their country," says Gracelyn Smallwood, the Aboriginal health expert whose arrest Dutton publicly defended in 2000.

Reconciliation is dead, but Peter Dutton is alive and kicking. In his perfect world, winners run countries. Losers write the history books.

In New South Wales, a backlash has been building against Labor's offshore windfarm policies. They are aiming to provide electricity to 4.2 million homes. Fake news circulates that the windfarms will kill four hundred whales a year. Barnaby Joyce addresses a 1500-strong rally in Port Stephens. "Cults don't listen to logic," says Joyce, "they just do whatever they like."

In the aftermath of the referendum, Peter Dutton makes a beeline for Nelson Bay. It is his second visit to the seat of Paterson in three weeks. His focus is Labor's coalmining electorates in regional New South Wales. Paterson voted 70 per cent No; Hunter was 71 per cent No. But Dutton isn't expecting the Voice alone to bring down this old Red Wall. Now he needs to cultivate an alternative moral high ground on climate change.

Dutton goes whale and dolphin watching with a Tackle World franchisee named Brent. Fifteen years ago, Dutton belittled Peter Garrett for lecturing him about how to raise his children. He told the Midnight Oil frontman to go back to worrying about the whales. The Opposition leader has seen the light. "When you look at, you know, the whales, and the mother and the calf that we saw out there; the dolphins," says Dutton. On the beach, the conviction is draining from his voice and face. "All of that is at risk."

Dutton wants to save the whales to save the tourism industry. He wants to save "rare bird species" too, and the lobster and marlin that fishermen catch to put food on the table for their families. He calls the wind farms "a national scandal." He accuses Labor of "absolute disregard" for its traditional voters. Locals have been "sold a pup." "What Chris Bowen is proposing to do here is to destroy the environment to save the planet."

Dutton travels south to the Central Coast. Traditional Howard battler territory. Labor holds Dobell and Robertson. They both voted No. Dutton visits Kulnura in the hinterland. Eastcoast Beverages is owned by a third-generation Italian migrant family. They started out by selling citrus at the Sydney Markets. Dutton does a tour of their farm. He says Labor should spend more time talking about Australia's migrant story, not just the sins against Aboriginals. "The modern Liberal Party is all about the Australian worker, about families, about people in suburbs, in regional towns."

The Central Coast is not a coalmining area, but residents are sensitive to rising electricity prices. Dutton doesn't deny climate change. Instead, he evangelises about the virtues of small nuclear modulators as a substitute for horizons scarred by wind and solar farms. This is starting to cut through. Polls show support for nuclear power is growing, particularly among younger voters, who weren't alive during the Cold War and the Chernobyl crisis.

"These guys talking about nuclear are in fantasy-land," says Matt Kean. He and many others believe that nuclear energy would increase power prices exponentially. Not to mention the time lag until functional nuclear modulators could be operating in Australia, even if public support could be obtained. Dutton is unperturbed. He isn't worried about the cost or the delay.

After visiting the Hunter Valley and the Central Coast, Dutton calls into 2GB for his weekly chinwag. Ray Hadley has a fixation with Chris Bowen. He plays Dutton a satirical spin on Bob Dylan's "Blowin' in the Wind."

> How many coal-fired plants must a man shut down before you can call him quite mad? And how many boats do you let sail in before your immigration goes bad? How many solar panels can you build anywhere before your electricity bill expands? Yes, and how many green wokey enthusiasts do you please by putting wind farms out at sea? And how many sea creatures will then fail to exist if you build this monstrosity? The answer, my friend, is Bowen and the wind.

"I don't know who scripted that," says Dutton, "but there's a special talent that's been utilised there to come up with those words. So, well done."

"Thanks very much," says Hadley. "I appreciate the praise."

Dutton is fighting windmills and chasing rainbows for dear life. He wants to save the whales and dolphins with uranium. It sounds like the environmental equivalent of his commitment to holding a second referendum.

*

Two days after the latest interest-rate rise, the High Court rules that indefinite immigration detention is unconstitutional. In 2012, "NZYQ" arrived in Australia by boat. He was a member of Myanmar's Rohingya people, a persecuted Muslim minority. He was eventually given a bridging visa. NZYQ was released to live in the western suburbs of Sydney. In January 2015, NZYQ anally raped a ten-year-old boy. It was eerily similar to the career-defining case that Peter Dutton investigated as a police officer. NZYQ was sentenced to five years in prison and released just three years later in 2018.

The immigration department cancelled NZYQ's bridging visa. He was detained indefinitely as an illegal non-citizen. Every country that Australia approached to resettle the man refused to take him. With the support of refugee advocates, NZYQ appealed to the High Court. His lawyer argued it was unconstitutional to detain someone with no prospect of deportation, based upon the argument that it was up to courts – not governments – to impose punishments. Most of the judges on the High Court agreed. NZYQ was released into the community. Albanese had been desperately trying to maintain a unity ticket with Dutton on immigration. Labor had no intention of ending indefinite detention. But the High Court forced its hand.

NZYQ would be followed to freedom by other "illegal non-citizens." Including Sirul Azhar Umar, a Malaysian hitman who assassinated a pregnant woman. And Aliyawar Yawari, an Afghan man convicted of sexually assaulting elderly Australian women. The main ethnicities of the freed? Afghan, Iranian, Iraqi and Sudanese. Rage transmits from tabloids and talkback radio to voters. The decision triggers all of Peter Dutton's visceral anger towards the judiciary and human rights advocates.

Shortly before Albanese's departure to America for an APEC meeting, Dutton launches all-out war. In Question Time, he sits opposite Albanese. They are unlikely rivals. Two warriors from the Hard Left and Hard Right of their respective parties. Yet they climbed, while the swankier stagnated or sank. Albanese has transformed from a tubby Tory fighter into a slim, well-mannered centrist. Dutton is balder and paunchier than his maiden speech. His broad frame fits that deep voice like a glove. The rims of his glasses are thick. Otherwise, the headkicker hasn't changed a bit.

Dutton asks the immigration minister, Andrew Giles, about the eighty-one "hardcore criminals" released into the community. Giles is a lawyer from Melbourne who acted as a solicitor for the asylum seekers on MV *Tampa*. Dutton is like a pitbull hunting a bunny rabbit. Giles clarifies that eighty-three people were released, actually. A charade ensues within the agitated parliament. Labor MPs ask Dorothy Dixers about bread-and-butter issues. The Coalition slowly turns up the blowtorch on Giles's belly. "Complying with the orders of the High Court is not optional," responds Giles, politely. "It is incumbent on this government and on any government."

Refusing to comply with judges and lawyers is the whole point of the Opposition leader's career. Power didn't corrupt or reveal Dutton. He has stayed true to the stubborn gut feelings that have always been on public display. Dutton moves a motion to suspend standing orders. He outlines a seven-point denunciation of the government. His voice rises from a mutter to a rumble. He bemoans the "breakdown in social cohesion" resulting from Labor's position on Israel and Palestine. He demands that Albanese convene a national cabinet to address the safety of Jewish citizens. "The dreadful attacks we saw on October 7 in Israel resulted in a … listed terrorist organisation … go in and massacre people of Jewish faith," says Dutton.

Next, Dutton links the outbreak of overseas extremism and domestic unrest to the release of stateless refugees from immigration detention centres. It is twenty-two years since *Tampa* and 9/11; eighteen years since the Cronulla Riots. For Dutton, this is all those situations rolled into one crisis. Like a pyromaniac, he pours petrol onto the bonfire of anxiety, while blaming Labor for the flames. In his version of events, the government personally decided to release the "hardened criminals" from immigration detention.

"Rapists!" shouts Dutton. "Paedophiles! Murderers!"

Disengaged voters are unlikely to wrap their heads around the intricacies of the High Court's decision, nor the geopolitical situation in the Middle East.

But they can wrap their heads around this: Arabs arriving by the carload in white beachside suburbs and dark-skinned rapists on the loose.

"One primary charge, as I say, for this prime minister," says Dutton, voice hoarse. "To keep the Australian public safe."

The connection between antisemitism and the High Court decision is confected. But the fear behind Dutton's outburst is sincere. His life moves anticlockwise. It is 1994. In his mind, eighty-three Sonny Grahams are now prowling the streets. Right before his eyes, Dutton can see Albanese morphing into Kim Beazley, the nice guy whom Howard accused of having no ticker. "This prime minister is as weak as water," says Dutton.

The feeling of déjà vu is mutual on Labor's backbench. After all that moral compromise with the horror of offshore detention, they are still getting creamed for being too soft. Within the Coalition, certain faces open with gleeful outrage. Some grow small with shame. "Prime Minister, don't leave this country until you have dealt with these issues," says Dutton. "Don't hop on the plane again to the United States."

Dutton's fists are clenched. He bangs the lectern for effect. For a second, it seems as if he is about to attempt a citizen's arrest; to handcuff Albanese to the desk. But Dutton sits down. Albanese prepares his riposte. This is one of the most important moments of his prime ministership. He condemns Dutton for the weaponisation of antisemitism. He waves an index finger. His brow is furrowed. If looks could kill, Dutton would be deceased. But Albanese doesn't wear seething anger quite so well as Dutton. It makes him seem fragile. His voice breaks. His bottom lip is quivering.

"[Leaders] have a choice: to either bring people together," says Albanese, "or divide them. Try to look for unity or look for opportunism. And what we have seen from this bloke here is consistent with his entire political career."

Dutton watches the character assassination impassively. A flicker of gratification crosses his face. He wants Albanese to wear his heart on his sleeve. Dutton's track record of bastardry is precisely what he is offering to the voters that he cares about. The world is a dangerous place, filled with evil strangers. Who do you want sticking up for you against them? A people-pleaser or a prick?

The Speaker calls for the doors to be locked. The tension dissipates. The politicians trudge like cattle to opposite sides of the parliament. Dutton's motion loses 54 votes to 86, but he won in the parliamentary morale stakes. Albanese flies to America, leaving behind a shattered backbench.

Deputy prime minister Richard Marles rushes through legislation to restrict the movements of the released men. Legal experts say the bill opens the government to the threat of multi-million-dollar compensation payouts. Dutton calls it too weak. A delegation of Labor MPs pays a visit to Dutton's office. He makes six suggestions to toughen the legislation. Labor accepts all of them carte blanche. "LABOR CRUMBLES … Humbled ALP backs in Peter's principles," reports the front page of *The Australian*.

It suits Dutton beautifully to be painted as a Trumpian outsider. As if he is a bug, not a fundamental feature of the political system. Dutton isn't anti-establishment. He *is* the establishment. There is barely a big issue where the policy settings aren't tilted more closely to his gut instincts.

*

A few days later, a boat carrying twelve people sails from Indonesia to the northern tip of Western Australia. Pakistani asylum seekers wander aimlessly through the crocodile-populated Kimberley, until they cross paths with a local Aboriginal mob. What do the two groups make of each other? Who is the bigger bane of Australia's existence? The lost refugees are taken to the Truscott–Mungalalo airstrip, a relic from World War II. Police arrive by helicopter to detain them. They are bound for a detention centre on Nauru.

That night, Dutton boards a chartered flight to Western Australia. But this has nothing to do with the asylum seekers. Gina Rinehart flies home from Bali on a $78-million G600 Gulfstream luxury jet. Australia's richest billionaire is hosting a "neon bush doof" at her Roy Hill Mine in the Pilbara. Dutton is flown to the shindig by WA billionaire Tim Roberts. The Opposition leader dons a high-vis pink vest for a happy snap with Rinehart.

At the party, a band entertains guests from the roof of a dump truck. Acrobats abound. Pauline Hanson is also in attendance. But Dutton is the undisputed guest of honour. Over dinner, Rinehart makes a speech inspired by Winston Churchill and Margaret Thatcher, the O.G. Iron Lady. She wants retirees to be able to work without their pensions being affected. "Where is the sense in restricting our own citizens from working while bringing in more immigrants when our hospitals already can't cope?" she asks.

Rinehart is worth $37.41 billion, up from $13.81 billion in 2019. She has done handsomely from the age of inequality. But the rage is being maintained. She calls for miners to get more of a voice via parliamentary representation. She implores supporters of the industry to spend at least fifteen minutes a day advocating her pecuniary interests. "Youngsters who've been to uni don't want to do work they think is below them … perhaps with the feeling that their private education or time at uni means they should pick and choose what work they do," she says.

Australia's cashless class war reaches the point of total psychosis. Rinehart – a university dropout – is joining the fight against the inner-city elite. She praises Dutton as an "outstanding leader." Dutton delivers a fawning tribute to his regular benefactor. He praises Rinehart's family as "pioneers" and the Roy Hill Mine as a "national treasure." "We need to hear more parents tell their children that the schools they attend, and the cities they live in, are only possible because of the mining sector," says Dutton.

Dutton offers acknowledgement to the mining industry. A smoking ceremony is performed for the traditional owner of the Coalition: Gina Rinehart. The leader of the Liberal Party tucks into some wagyu brisket and ribs. This is Dutton in a nutshell. He kisses up and punches down.

Overnight, news breaks about the arrival of the twelve asylum seekers. Border Force officials fly them to Nauru. Peter Dutton goes back to Brisbane for a meeting with Bravehearts, a child sexual abuse advocacy group. Afterwards, Dutton holds a press conference. He criticises the suspicious swiftness of Labor's decision to set aside visas for Palestinian refugees.

"We need to make sure that people who are coming out of a war zone don't pose a threat to Australian citizens," he says. "We've seen before … [Labor] go out with a program that they want people to believe is big-hearted and they're on higher moral ground … and the Liberal Party's too tough."

None of the journalists ask him about the recent visit to lick ribs with Gina Rinehart, or if this contradicts his vilification of wealthy elites. The questions are about pornography, war, immigration and boat people. It isn't a complete conspiracy. His fixations neatly overlap with issues that sell newspapers and attract TV viewers, a self-perpetuating cycle of anxiety.

"What we know from this prime minister is that he stopped the economy and he started the boats," says Dutton, smelling blood. "The people smugglers see Anthony Albanese as a soft touch because he is a soft touch."

Dutton believes that Australians are starting to see Albanese as the friendly yes-man they can't afford during an emergency. He believes enough people will prefer, deep down, for the country to be run by him: the naysayer. It certainly wouldn't be the first time that an anxious nation wet the bed about the Labor Party and embraced a garden-variety hardman to clean the sheets.

The next day, Dutton attends the state convention for the NSW Liberal Party in Sydney. Protestors in hazmat suits and breathing masks address Dutton as the Member for Fukushima. "Nukes R Us," they chant. The event is titled "A New Hope." Some true believers boo during the Acknowledgement of Country. Dutton pays tribute to Robert Menzies, the Forgotten People and moderate Liberal George Brandis. "[George] will mop up any of the difficulties or problems or inaccuracies that I've delivered in my speech – so thank you, George," says Dutton, just joshing.

Dutton is buoyed by focus-group feedback. Australians are getting feral about Albanese. Reconciliation is dead. The boats are back. The Monkey Pod was patient. Now, the good old days are nigh. "I notice there's been some media speculation around what my two-term strategy might be," says Dutton. "There is no two-term strategy. Our strategy is one term."

A Newspoll is published Sunday night, 23 November 2023. Labor and the Coalition are 50–50, narrowing from 57–43 in September 2022. Dutton's net satisfaction rating is –13, the same as Albanese's. The prime minister is down from +35 in July 2022. People don't love Dutton. But he isn't as diabolically unpopular as some assume. Abbott won after plummeting to –36. This is the wedge-and-win strategy. The wrecker doesn't necessarily get full credit for their effectiveness. It is a long way to the top. Abbott was in a much stronger starting position. The Coalition has significant new structural defects. Labor might tame the cost-of-living crisis. Here is a hot tip: Dutton will leave nothing to destiny. He knows that power only comes to those who pounce.

January 2024 delivers the annual debate about Australia Day. Peter Dutton gets on the front foot. Woolworths announces that it will no longer be selling Chinese-made Australia Day merchandise, citing a lack of consumer demand. Dutton accuses Woolworths of signing up to Albanese's "woke agenda" and being more focused on fighting culture wars than the cost of living. "I think Australians should boycott Woolworths," he says.

This is a key ingredient of the Suburban Strategy. Dutton is attempting to airbrush the Liberal Party's association with big business. Working-class Woolworths employees are collateral damage. They are abused by angry patriots. In Brisbane, a man graffities a Woolworths store: *5 days 26 Jan Aussie Oi Oi Woolies Fuck U. Boycott Woolies.* He sets off a flare under the front door. Dutton lights the fuse with his words and then goes AWOL. A poll by YouGov shows that only 20 per cent of Australians back his call for a boycott. Fourteen per cent support Woolworths' decision. Sixty-six per cent state that their main priority is "excessive price rises rather than this issue."

The Opposition leader has perhaps learnt the wrong lesson from the referendum. A lot of disengaged No voters were not signing up for a 24/7 "war on woke." They were disenchanted by the lack of focus on the cost of living, and the intrusion of acrimonious political issues into their lives. Dutton is offering them the division of the Voice campaign on a permanent basis.

"The Forgotten People don't give a tinker's cuss about culture wars," Liberal MP Bridget Archer tells me. "They're not Team Red. They're not Team Blue. They just want to feel that you understand their struggles."

Meanwhile, Albanese tries to make peace with the outer-suburban and regional voters who deserted Labor during the Voice campaign. The prime minister breaks his constant promise not to fiddle with the stage three tax cuts. He revises them to benefit low- and middle-income earners. Albanese's backflip provides Dutton with an opportunity to put his money where his mouth is. But old habits die hard. "The government's rewriting of stage three will hinder aspiration, crush confidence and obliterate opportunity," he says.

The Liberals' deputy leader, Sussan Ley, pledges to "absolutely" overturn Labor's changes to the tax cuts. Then she accuses Labor of lying about her pledge. The Coalition backtracks and vacillates. This is quite a pickle. The winners are heavily concentrated in Peter Dutton's target seats, such as Dunkley, the outer-suburban Melbourne seat where a byelection is imminent. The losers are heavily concentrated in the inner-metropolitan seats that the Liberals lost at the last election. Dutton has spent the past year courting the winners and ignoring or actively antagonising the losers.

At a press conference, Dutton's voice is unusually high-pitched. He is visibly flustered. He accuses Albanese – "a smart political operator" – of attempting to wedge the Coalition before the upcoming Dunkley byelection. Judging by his response, the wedge was planted in a sensitive place.

"[Albanese] lies to the Australian public," says Dutton. "He doesn't have the guts to stand up and say that he believes in Australia Day."

Dutton is uncommitted to bigger tax cuts for nurses and truck drivers. But he does want to legislate Australia Day. Presented with a platform for a serious debate about tax reform and inflation, Dutton ricochets like a pinball into culture wars. On the eve of Australia Day, Dutton and Jacinta Price publish a joint letter. They want to make Australia great again. The country has become too obsessed with the bloodshed of the past. Too eager to belittle the British Empire. "Everyday Australians have had a gutful of elites seeking to crush our national pride, tear down the Australian achievement and tribalise us through every form of identity politics," they write.

Dutton is Australia's pre-eminent practitioner of right-wing identity politics. He highlights difference for a living. His career has been spent persuading Australians to prioritise cultural belonging above egalitarianism.

Under pressure, Dutton tries to change the subject. He takes aim at two of his favourite punching bags: lawyers and journalists. He promises to defund the Environmental Defenders Office, a legal centre offering assistance to climate change cases. Meanwhile, *Guardian Australia*'s political editor, Katharine Murphy, announces she is leaving the press gallery for a job in the office of the prime minister. "I am genuinely shocked to see

Murpharoo take up a spot to now be officially be running lines for Labor," tweets Dutton. "The real outrage is David Crowe missed out. What more must he do to prove his credentials to be formally employed by the Labor Party?" Murphy has been one of Dutton's most vocal critics. Crowe's crime was not reporting on changes to the stage three tax cuts with the same breathless hyperbole as Ray Hadley.

Dutton is a hard man with a glass jaw. He feels entitled to the highest prize of Australian democracy, yet he resents attention and accountability. His siege mentality gets exhausting. You are with him or at war with him. Ultimately, this might be the side of Dutton that disengaged voters come to like the least as they start to pay more attention. The petty obsession with what Scott Morrison breezily dismissed as "the Canberra bubble." For Dutton, everything is political. Nobody is off-limits, except for him.

*

John Howard turned the Australian dream into a pyramid scheme. Dutton is running a protection racket for the winners. He is one of them. In 2020, the Duttons sold their Camp Mountain home for $1.8 million. They bought a $2.165-million farm. A year later, the Gold Coast mansion was sold for $6 million. The humble suburban man purchased a $2.7-million penthouse in the Brisbane CBD. He flipped it the next year for $3.47 million.

"[Labor] don't understand the reality of what normal people do in terms of their budgeting and way in which they live their lives," Dutton tells Ray Hadley, following a rant about the Voice and "woke CEOs."

Dutton launches a scare campaign about negative gearing and capital gains. The wedges are endless. He accuses Labor of secretly pursuing "Robin Hood" economics: robbing from the rich to give to the poor. Robin Hood's nemesis was the Sheriff of Nottingham, a much-maligned autocrat who collected taxes for the aristocracy.

"If [Labor] come out and say that we're going to cap negative gearing or abolish negative gearing or change capital gains arrangements, all they'll do is kill confidence in the economy," says Dutton.

On stage three tax cuts, Dutton doesn't maintain the rage. The Coalition agrees to pass Labor's legislation. It is too obviously popular with the silent majority. Dutton is a self-styled conviction politician. He initially called for an election over the broken promise. Now he is joining a unity ticket with "the liar in the Lodge." At a press conference, Dutton expresses concern about the economic pressures on single parents and homeless people. "We are the parties of the working class," he says.

So far, the main solution that Dutton has offered to the housing crisis is to allow first homebuyers to gut their superannuation accounts for mortgage deposits. He would do this while reimbursing the extra $2 billion a year that Labor is collecting from higher taxes on superannuation accounts over $3 million. The franking credits of wealthy retirees are off-limits. But the nest eggs of millennials are fair game to keep the property market booming in perpetuity. Dutton has also repeatedly made vague suggestions that he would cut immigration. "They're bringing in … some 500,000 people," he says today. "The housing stock is not keeping up with the number of arrivals."

Dutton is a scarecrow grasping for a straw man argument. He is trying to make migrants – not landlords – the main enemy of angry renters. Then he goes on a rant about the "dodgy" renewable energy projects of merchant bankers. His target is clear: the previous night, Malcolm Turnbull called Dutton a "thug." "Have you found me to be a thug?" Dutton asks a journalist.

There is an emotional component to Dutton's inflexibility on negative gearing and capital gains. This is what he knows best: buy homes, flip them and get rich. The bruiser from Boondall is irked by insinuations that the wealth of suburban property investors is less well earned than that of cosmopolitan merchant bankers. But he refuses to bite back at the former prime minister, saying, "I can only deal with one liar at a time."

In Question Time, Dutton flogs Albanese with a wet lettuce. A week ago, the Coalition were accusing the prime minister of perpetrating the greatest lie in modern Australian politics. Today, they have no queries about the changes to the stage three tax cuts. Instead, Dutton asks Albanese to rule out modifications to negative gearing and capital gains. The prime minister is glowing and grinning. Dutton is a shell of his November self.

The lesson for Labor? The Sheriff of Nottingham never won any popularity contests against Robin Hood. Dutton needs to be tested, not placated. He is an opportunist who only responds to electoral pressure. The best weapon against right-wing culture wars is proper social democracy.

*

That night, Dutton makes a grudging appearance on ABC TV's 7.30. He is stiff in his skin. There is more to this bland man than meets the eye. No doubt and so much dread. His line of sight is small. His will to win is big. But he wants to be the prime minister without people seeing him.

Presenter Sarah Ferguson asks the alternative prime minister some blunt questions about the backflip on tax cuts. Dutton bristles. He senses a conspiracy.

"Well, Sarah, I don't think it's your job to push the position of the government," says Dutton.

"It's absolutely not; this is an outside observer—" says Ferguson.

"I wish it was," Dutton interjects.

Ferguson presents analysis contesting his. This is her job. He frames it as "praise" of Labor. This is Dutton's paranoid style. He finds safety in the echo chamber of talkback radio and *Sky After Dark*. There he can avoid true scrutiny, like a vampire shying away from sunlight. Ferguson probes him on Turnbull's accusation of thuggery. Dutton counter-accuses the impartial national broadcaster of harbouring a "far left" bias. He tells the ABC to stop living in the ancient past of the last decade.

"I don't think anyone's scared of ghosts," he says, lips cracked. "I think everyone moves on. And I think – frankly – the Australian public has so moved on from that era it's not funny." By the end of the argument, Dutton has had a change of heart about a fresh start: "I'm very much shaped by the Howard and Costello era when I first came into parliament. I was the assistant treasurer."

Dutton has a complicated relationship with history. He is appalled and enthralled by it. He is forever riding a time machine to 2001. The glory days when men like him were getting rich quick. When dole bludgers were bigger public enemies than landlords. When America was the only superpower. When elections could be won on boat people and Islamic terrorism. When First Nations people were treated as a law-and-order issue. Dutton wants a country where people don't worry about the powerful and feel threatened by the defenceless. He thinks this is enough to win.

"This is a government that's rattled and the wheels are coming off," he told Sky News in late 2023. "And this is a weak and woke prime minister."

This is Peter Dutton. Tall and strong at first glance. But when you watch him for a long time, you can see that the man is small and scared.

SOURCES

Peter Dutton and his office didn't respond to interview requests. Many interviews for the essay were on background or off the record. There are direct quotes from Bridget Archer, Cheryl Kernot, Wyatt Roy, Andrew Bragg, Malcolm Turnbull, George Brandis, Robin Carter, Bob Katter, Matt Kean, Keith Wolahan, Maria Kovacic and Tony Barry.

Sources include:

"Conservatives, comedians and political correctness", *Q&A*, ABC, 15 March 2010.
"Defining Dutton", *Four Corners*, ABC TV, 26 September 2022.
"Peter Dutton", *Kitchen Cabinet*, ABC TV, 22 August 2023.

Jeannine Smith and Peter Craig Dutton, District Court, Appeal no. 4870 of 1997, 3 March 1998.
Peter Craig Dutton v. Bradley John Bell, District Court, Case D5016 of 2000, 15 April 2003.
The Queen v. Sonny Paul Graham, Court of Appeal, CA number 324 of 1995, 23 October 1995.

"Dutton encourages community input on new curriculum", *Gatton, Lockyer and Brisbane Valley Star*, 10 March 2010.
"Dutton plays 'Baste the Bear'," *Queensland Figaro and Punch*, 23 July 1887, p. 2.
"Home truths" series, *The Sydney Morning Herald*, 2023–2024.
"The late Captain Coley", *The Queensland Times*, 1864.
"Select Committee into the Native Police", report, 1861.
"Throwing over the poor man", *The Queenslander*, 4 October 1884.
"Trafficked" series, *The Sydney Morning Herald*, 2022.

Albrechtsen, Janet, "The bonfire of cash: The small motley No crew that beat Yes", *The Australian*, 15 October 2023.
Bates, Cameron, "Townsville Indigenous leader Gracelyn Smallwood reacts to Voice loss", *The Townsville Bulletin*, 15 October 2023.
Bottoms, Timothy, *Conspiracy of Silence*, Allen & Unwin, 2013.
Bramston, Troy, "No regrets: a hard man with the right stuff", *The Australian*, 13 November 2021.
Brett, Judith, *Robert Menzies' Forgotten People*, Melbourne University Press, 2007.
Butler, Josh, "Peter Dutton was flown by a billionaire to Gina Rinehart's Pilbara party", *Guardian Australia*, 10 January 2024.
Button, James, "Dutton's dark victory", *The Monthly*, February 2018.
Cameron, Peter, "Dutton dilemma", *Gold Coast Bulletin*, 6 October 2009.

Cole, Malcolm, "Running against history", *The Courier Mail*, 29 September 2003.

Di Stefano, Mark, "Gina Rinehart handholds Peter Dutton at her neon bush doof", *Australian Financial Review*, 23 November 2023.

Di Stefano, Mark, "It looks like we've found Peter Dutton's great-great-grandfather", *Buzzfeed*, 22 May 2016.

Crowe, David, *Venom*, HarperCollins, 2019.

Dutton, Peter, "Jail sisters spoil the Hanson party", *The Sun-Herald*, 16 November 2003.

Dutton, Peter, "Patching society's cracked foundation", *The Courier Mail*, 30 December 2003.

Dutton, Peter and Steve Ciobo, "Is it a question of identity?", *The Courier Mail*, 20 July 2005.

Evans, Raymond and Robert Ørsted-Jensen "'I cannot say the numbers that were killed': Assessing violent mortality on the Queensland frontier", 19 July 2014, available at https://papers.ssrn.com/sol3/papers.cfm? abstract_id=2467836.

Farr, Malcolm, "Liberal MP leads nanny state rebellion", *The Daily Telegraph*, 21 August 2008.

Franklin, Matthew, "Messenger takes flak for prime minister", *The Courier Mail*, 11 November 2005.

Frenkel, Jason, "Disabled told to get jobs", *Herald Sun*, 25 November 2005.

Gibson, Ross, *Seven Versions of an Australian Badland*, UQP, 2002.

Glasgow, Will and Christine Lacy, "Why gearing gets a hearing from Peter Dutton", *The Australian*, 2 December 2016.

Gothe-Snape, Jackson, "Divided by politics but united by trauma", ABC, 10 May 2019.

Hartcher, Peter, "Albanese had been underestimated his whole life. Then he overestimated himself", *The Sydney Morning Herald*, 21 October 2023.

Karvelas, Patricia "ABC rents from minister", *The Australian*, 4 April 2006.

Karvelas, Patricia, "Dole plan takes axe to soft options", *The Australian*, 11 June 2005.

Kemp, C.D., "Menzies and the middle class", Institute of Public Affairs, 1 October 1992.

King, Madonna, "Good Cop, Bad Cop", *Good Weekend*, 9 August 2014.

Knox, Malcolm, "The Makeover: Peter Dutton's hard sell to the electorate", *The Monthly*, November 2022.

Lawrence, Elissa, "How Brisbane mother Ali France overcame it all", *The Courier Mail*, 18 March 2018.

Leavers, Ian, "Woke obsession needs to stop as police hands are tied", *The Courier Mail*, 25 October 2023.

Maiden, Samantha, "Dutton likely to play bad cop on health", *Sunday Mail*, 9 February 2014.

Marr, David, *Killing for Country*, Black Inc., 2023.

Massola, James and Anthony Galloway, "Dutton concedes Liberal Party in an 'identity crisis', willing to deal with the teals", *The Sydney Morning Herald*, 4 December 2022.

McConnel, Katherine, *Our Wayward and Backward Sister Colony: Queensland and the Australian Federation Movement 1859–1901*, University of Queensland, 2006.

McKenna, Michael, "Kernot caught out in poll mud-slinging", *The Courier Mail*, 12 October 2001.

O'Regan, Sylvia Varnham, "Why New Zealand is furious about Australia's deportation policies", *The New York Times*, 3 July 2018."

Price, Matt, "PM's wunderkind turns up only on hubris", *The Australian*, 31 March 2006.

Pyne, Christopher, *The Insider*, Hachette, 2020.

Rabe, Tom and Brad Thomson, "Send miners to parliament and students to work, Gina Rinehart says", *Australian Financial Review*, 22 November 2023.

Shanahan, Dennis, "Liberal voting heartland is shifting to the 'outer suburbs'", *The Australian*, 24 May 2022.

Snow, Deborah, "Peter Dutton: I'm just not impacted by that hatred", *Good Weekend*, 23 May 2017.

Reynolds, Henry, *This Whispering in Our Hearts Revisited*, NewSouth Publishing, 2018. Reynolds, Henry, *Truth-Telling*, NewSouth Publishing, 2021.

Savva, Niki, *Plots and Prayers*, Scribe, 2019.

Turnbull, Malcolm, *A Bigger Picture*, Hardie Grant, 2020.

Viellaris, Renee, "Fighting spirit behind 'Minister for Misery'", *The Courier Mail*, 21 August 2018.

Viellaris, Renee, "Peter Dutton unleashes on Malcolm Turnbull", *The Courier Mail*, 30 December 2018.

Visentin, Lisa, "From juvie to supermax to despair", *The Sydney Morning Herald*, 27 September 2015.

Whitton, Evan, *The Hillbilly Dictator*, ABC Books, 1989.

Whyte, Sarah, "Tough talking Dutton promises guns for border protection staff", *The Sunday Age*, 31 December 2014.

Wardill, Steven, "Minister failed to make the grade", *The Courier Mail*, 27 January 2006.

THE GREAT DIVIDE

Correspondence

Nicole Haddow

In his essay *The Great Divide*, Alan Kohler defines my tribe, the millennial generation, as anyone who was born after Bonnie Tyler's "Total Eclipse of the Heart" was a number-one hit. Having entered the world just as 1982 made way for 1983, I consider myself to be an ageing millennial matriarch with first-hand experience of the problems highlighted in Kohler's essay and therefore feel qualified to provide this correspondence.

Kohler observes that the year 2000 was the dawn of the "Great Divide" in housing. I turned eighteen at the end of that year and was far too busy enjoying the new freedoms that came with a driver's licence and the ability to order a drink at the pub to be concerned with the matter of property. I intended to work hard, and the past had assured me that anyone who worked hard enough could buy a house when they were ready for such a commitment.

I was wrong. During the years that I heartily indulged in my youth and enjoyed the share house rite of passage, the market was shifting rapidly. By the time I moved out of my final share house on the eve of my thirtieth birthday, in 2012 – having handed over tens of thousands of dollars to landlords while trying to build my career – the median house price in Melbourne was about $530,000, more than seven times my annual salary at that point. And I was single, so buying solo felt impossible.

As Kohler explains, this has remained a challenge, with median house prices still at 7.4 times annualised average weekly earnings. In my case, cracking the property market meant making two critical decisions: moving home with my parents to do a "power save" at thirty, and ultimately purchasing an apartment at a price point that was significantly lower than the median dwelling price.

Kohler is right that the cost of housing is a serious problem in Australia, but more attention should be applied to what I believe is the biggest barrier to entry: saving a deposit. Most banks require a 20 per cent deposit along with additional costs.

A 20 per cent deposit on the median $732,886 price that Kohler calls out is $146,577. And that's just the deposit. Even if a first homebuyer or couple did manage to save that 20 per cent, once you add more than $39,000 in stamp duty, about $2000 in government costs, $1000 for conveyancing plus mortgage set-up fees, the would-be buyer(s) only have a 14 per cent deposit. Their loan-to-value ratio would be 86 per cent, making them a risky prospect as far as the bank is concerned; they'd therefore be slapped with a Lenders Mortgage Insurance (LMI) charge of approximately $9000, which protects the bank in the event of a default, not the customer. That "insurance" would likely be capitalised into the life of the loan, costing them a stack of additional interest for as long as they held the property.

In my view, the way that loans are structured is outdated and needs urgent review in light of the cost of entering the market. Kohler says that many young people may access the Bank of Mum and Dad to cover deposit shortfalls, but if you don't have that (I didn't), chances are you'll cop the LMI rather than saving the full 20 per cent plus costs (this is what I did). I justified the LMI by putting a strategy in place that could benefit me in the long run. This meant buying an established apartment 25 kilometres from Melbourne's CBD for about $300,000 with a deposit of less than 10 per cent in a red-brick block of just six. It was, frankly, pretty crap. But it was in a growing suburb, in a wide street full of nice homes, close to amenities. I hoped that it would rise in value over the course of six to eight years and enable me to take my next step into a freestanding home. Not in Melbourne, of course, don't be ridiculous.

My second step up the property ladder came with a not-so-gentle shove from the pandemic. At the time, I was renting in the inner city and had a tenant in my property. They moved out during the first lockdown, leaving me covering both my own rent and a mortgage on an empty apartment. Thanks to a fortunate break in the form of a mortgage pause, I was able to sell the property and make a profit that would provide enough funds to purchase something larger. At that time, forty was looming and I wanted a permanent home. To secure one on a single income, I had to look beyond the city to regional Victoria, which was feasible only because I had the benefit of remote work.

I bought in Ballarat, 115 kilometres west of Melbourne. While I was proud to have finally made a successful offer on a weatherboard cottage, I was also moving away from family and friends. This was early in 2021. I knew no one. Snap lockdowns continued to hit throughout my first year there. I was desperately lonely, but this was the price I believed I needed to pay for my future security. Thanks to record low interest rates and wild demand for dwellings outside of the most locked-down city in the world, that price was high. My budget afforded me a property with a hole in the bedroom floor, some unplastered walls and one entirely inadequate heater for the frosty climate. But again, I bought with the dual purpose of secure accommodation and the potential for growth. I knew I could add value and make it an attractive asset if I ever needed to sell.

A year in, I'd painted and made several improvements, and for the first time in a long time I felt that I was finally getting ahead. And then, surprise! Thirteen interest rate rises. Cheers, RBA. I understood the emergency interest rates would eventually lift but never anticipated being hit this frequently this fast. Today my mortgage is about $1400 more than it was when I purchased the home. However, just as the hikes kicked off, I met the man who became my husband. He has not only made Ballarat home, he's also enabled us to weather the cost-of-living battle together. Had our paths not crossed, I would be under extreme mortgage stress.

Kohler's essay paints a clear and empathetic picture of the many struggles aspiring buyers and new entrants to the market face today. But the cost of property is only one piece of the greater social puzzle for millennials and the generations that follow. My husband and I are incredibly privileged to have two incomes, and that I managed to purchase our property at below the state's median price in 2021. Our children are of the fur variety, and while we need to allow for food and occasional medical expenses, we do not bear the financial burden of paid care or education.

How can any young couple – without access to the Bank of Mum and Dad – not only save for a deposit, but then go on to cover the cost of a mortgage, bills, food and childcare? How do they manage costs when one parent must step out of the workforce for extended parental leave? Currently, parental leave is approximately $880 per week for just twenty weeks, and while parents will enjoy up to twenty-six weeks of paid leave by 2026, this small sum does not come close to compensating those shouldering the combined costs of early family life. The parent who takes on the primary caring role is also missing out on superannuation during that time, and potentially making this sacrifice intermittently for years, depending on the number of children they have.

Our support for young families is pitiful when compared with that in other nations. In Finland, each parent is entitled to 160 days of paid leave (more than fourteen months in total). The average across OECD nations in late 2022 was 50.8. Even when Australian primary carers do return to work, they must find a way to manage employment and care for their babies. Anecdotally, I know couples who are spending over $20,000 per year on childcare alone. The combined costs mean that raising a family is turning from a fairly reasonable dream into a luxury.

I believe many growing families will be forced to do what I did, moving a long way from their roots to the end of train lines and beyond for "reasonable" mortgages. If this trend continues, other social shifts must occur, including ongoing acceptance of work-from-home practices, strong employment opportunities and increased investment in outer-suburban and regional infrastructure, not just more housing.

Property prices are causing more than a great divide; there is now a cavernous gap between those who own their home and those who do not. I worry not just about our present circumstances but about how my generation will fare at retirement age. How will we accommodate everyone who was not fortunate enough to secure a home? A roof over one's head should be a right, not a privilege. Yet, as Kohler points out, if most people have a vested interest in property prices rising for their own security, little will change.

The number-one hitmaker of 1983 was right when she sang, "Every now and then I get a little bit nervous / That the best of all the years have gone by." Don't those of us who were born at that time or in the years that followed know it.

Nicole Haddow

Joseph Walker

For many years, I've been waiting for somebody to write the canonical treatment of Australia's housing mess. Maybe a young Aussie Robert Caro would emerge and take a microscope to every corner of what is becoming our most urgent public policy problem. Such an account would no doubt amount to the literary equivalent of urban sprawl.

The Great Divide is neither canonical, such is the nature of word limits, nor is Alan Kohler, after a long and distinguished career in finance journalism, a millennial. But his Quarterly Essay is sober, necessary and broadly correct in its conclusions; and perhaps its message is best conveyed by a baby boomer like Kohler, whose vision is anchored in memories of a more functional past.

It is a fact of life that the cost of the structures we live in – or, more accurately, the land under them – keeps going up, even as the prices of the stuff we fill them with keep coming down. Over the past twenty-three years, house price-to-income ratios have doubled, from 3.5 to seven. According to the 2023 Demographia report, Sydney and Melbourne are the second and ninth least affordable cities on Earth.

Something that should be a national shame is, judging by the popularity of real estate TV and the size of crowds at weekend auctions, actually a national sport. As a friend quipped to me: America is number one in the world in health-care costs, and it's a disaster; Australia is (almost) number one in housing costs, and it's celebrated.

So, what started the party? Or at least: what set off the most recent boom? The capital gains tax discount, Kohler answers. On my podcast in 2020, I discussed this possibility with Nobel Prize–winning economist Vernon Smith. As Smith explained, the story in the United States was similar; he identified the *Taxpayer Relief Act* of 1997, Clinton's act, which exempted from capital gains taxes the first $500,000 of any home sale, as the trigger for the US housing bubble.

Howard's 50 per cent discount was even more investor-friendly. By sweetening the deal on the resale value of housing, the effect of the tax break in Australia, as in the US, was to shift perceptions of what could be achieved with property.

For all this, Kohler's astute historical analysis bleeds into a dubious economic argument; he writes as if the CGT discount is one of the – if not the – most important drivers of prices at *current margins* – a separate and less substantiated claim (indeed, a claim incompatible with some of the other research he cites).

If the CGT discount lit the spark, what has been fuelling the blaze? Kohler gives a comprehensive if not complete accounting of the myriad factors that have been swelling demand or dampening supply (missing, for example, are foreign investors). Haunting his analysis of the demand side are Australia's one-million-strong negatively geared property speculators.

Kohler does not, however, get sidetracked in circular debates about bubbles.

This is just as well. Demand and supply are like the blades on a pair of scissors. Prices are set not by one half or the other but by their interaction. A corollary of this basic economic insight is that even if demand-side changes have been the proximate cause of the price rises of recent decades, as they surely have, their impact can be absorbed by the supply side.

In principle, that is. In practice, Australia's housing supply is chronically inelastic.

If Kohler's essay has a flaw, it's that he doesn't prosecute his own argument vigorously enough. He outlines the obvious or first-order harms of high house prices, namely declining home ownership, a "lack of security" and, importantly, rising inequality. But beyond that, his treatment of the downside risks is cursory. Two pages are given to discussing the decline of pet ownership among renters – a sad trend, to be sure, but in that passage he spills as much ink on cats and dogs (552 words) as on three of the worst repercussions of housing unaffordability: crippled productivity, macroeconomic fragility and falling fertility (553 words). It's worth underscoring these harms in turn (to say nothing of the many other ills of housing unaffordability, such as the misery of long commutes and the environmental damage wrought by urban sprawl).

First, high house prices in our major cities stunt national productivity. Cities are engines of entrepreneurship. They facilitate specialisation and the sharing of information (what economists call "knowledge spillover effects"). As Ed Glaeser puts it in *Triumph of the City*, "ideas cross corridors and streets more easily than continents and seas." By pricing our fellow citizens out of our most productive places, we don't just deprive them of better wages; we deny our country greater wealth.

Second, high house prices make us macroeconomically fragile. In particular, excessive household debt coupled with high house prices render the risk of a balance sheet recession – the nastiest form of recession – at least plausible.

Australia has the second-highest household debt-to-GDP ratio in the world. Most of that debt is tied up in residential mortgages. While much less of our mortgage debt is held by subprime borrowers than was the case in the United States, marginal propensities to consume out of housing wealth don't approach 0 until closer to the top 10 per cent of the income distribution anyway, according to research by economists Amir Sufi and Atif Mian. That is, 90 per cent of income earners can still be expected to tighten their belts if prices collapsed. So, we're not exempt from this risk, however robust our position may seem.

Third, expensive housing is preventing couples who want to have kids, or have more kids, from having them. Children usually need bedrooms, and every extra bedroom means a bigger mortgage.

At the individual level, this is frustrating. At the societal level, it's disastrous. As Kohler notes, our fertility rate is already below replacement level. This seeds structural imbalances wherein fewer workers must support more retirees. It undercuts productivity: our best economic growth models imply that population growth drives technological progress (since more minds means more Einsteins). And it frays the thread connecting society to its future – a condition that, unlike the others, can't be postponed by mass immigration.

High house prices are a plague not just in Australia but across the Anglosphere. Indeed, their consequences are both so perverse and so pervasive that housing advocate John Myers and economists Sam Bowman and Ben Southwood coined a term, "the housing theory of everything," to explain how housing unaffordability undergirds so much of the deep dysfunction we observe in the West.

What can be done? *The Great Divide* is really an essay about three great divides, all of which have conspired to put solutions out of reach. The first is the titular divide, between those who own homes and those who do not. For most Australian homeowners, housing forms the greater portion of their wealth. Since losses loom larger than gains psychologically, this group resists policies that put their nest eggs at risk with a passionate intensity that can't be matched by aspiring homeowners.

Proposals for reducing house prices that are not accompanied by compensation to these owner-occupiers for lost equity – however undeserved that equity may be – are unlikely to shake the "generational tyranny" of the boomers (or the resistance of younger people who have managed to buy into the homeownership club before prices rose).

The second divide is between local residents and would-be residents. Local zoning rules, such as they are, give cranky NIMBY residents effective veto rights over new construction in their neighbourhoods.

There is an imbalance. Locals have both the capacity and the incentive to block new development. They can coordinate easily because they're both physically proximate and few in number. And their reasons for enforcing the status quo, ranging from risk aversion to heritage preservationism (sincere or otherwise), are powerfully motivating.

On the other hand, non-residents looking to rent or buy in a city area would hypothetically be YIMBYs, but how can they organise to express their preferences? They're spread across a city, or outside of it, if they even think of themselves as potential residents of a particular area at all. Moreover, the housing affordability costs of any one development not getting built are thinly spread and provide inadequate impetus for these strangers to overcome their coordination problems.

This entrenches a fallacy of composition that hobbles efforts to increase housing supply. Any one rejection of new construction by NIMBYs at the local level may be both comprehensible and negligible. But scaled up to the national level, all those local decisions sum up to a housing shortage.

The third divide is, as Kohler laments, between two political impulses. The housing problem has become an ideological Rorschach test, in which the left, with its focus on equality, blames demand-side greed, whereas the right, with its belief in markets, prefers supply-side explanations.

But there are signs that the third divide – and hence the second – can be bridged. There is growing recognition on the political left that zoning is inherently inegalitarian. In the United States, liberals such as Ezra Klein and Derek Thompson have begun pushing for a "supply-side progressivism," wherein the left redirects some of its energies from the demand side of the ledger to the creation of goods and services; in Klein's words, it's the "stupidly simple" thesis that "to have the future we want, we need to build and invent more of the things that we need." Above all, that includes housing.

This new "abundance agenda", with its wide political promise, is instantiated Down Under in the bipartisan YIMBY groups that have recently sprouted in Canberra, Sydney, Brisbane and Melbourne, and in their new alliance to form the Abundant Housing Network Australia.

There are pockets of hope, but a broad will is necessary to transform the housing situation. Can such consensus be found? I sense a deep pessimism on Kohler's part. Given the seeming irreconcilability of the three divides, such pessimism is understandable!

But if we're bound to fail anyway, why not permit ourselves to fantasise a little? How about land value taxes, like the Georgists have long argued? Kohler dismisses these out of hand, but taxing the gains – or rents – of agglomeration could be a highly efficient way to redistribute revenue to, for example, the regions – to say nothing of its ethical justification. Speaking of the regions, why not found new cities – or transform Darwin into an Australian Singapore – as Ken Henry suggested to me in 2023? Or if that's too audacious, can we not turn to the age-old saviour: technology? Just as trains and cars opened up effective supply in the nineteenth and twentieth centuries, perhaps Zoom and virtual reality will do the same in the twenty-first. With the rise of working from home, can we convert office space into residential? To address the problem of the "missing middles", why not allow street-level votes for gentle density, as has been proposed by YIMBY groups in England and Ireland – a win-win solution that can dissolve the second great divide? Or how about establishing home equity insurance markets, as Bob Shiller has proposed, to placate the NIMBY "homevoters"?

For Kohler, no solution is tenable until we purge ourselves of the belief that "house prices always rise and that housing is the best way to build wealth." Ideally, we would engineer a flatlining of prices for the next eighteen years, until incomes catch up. A hard landing is off the table – wise, given the balance sheet recession risk.

Kohler is right that we must dislodge property from its pedestal, though this raises the question of whether the desired soft landing would be self-defeating. If speculators, already bleeding rental losses, then no longer expect capital gains, why wouldn't they just try to sell – threatening a mass exit that could crash prices?

There is also the question of political will. Any attempted normalisation of prices by policymakers needs to be orchestrated with an heroic gradualism that outlives election cycles and the political temptations of pumping home equity.

But these nagging questions give way to a deeper one. Howard's throwaway comment on ABC Radio in 2003 ("I haven't had anybody shake their fist at me and say: 'Howard, I'm angry with you for letting the value of my house increase'") hints at a strange connection between our fixation on property and our lackadaisical attitude to productivity.

In an age of rising income inequality and stagnating productivity growth, have debt and equity become a palliative in Australia, as Raghuram Rajan argues they have in the US since the 1970s?

Thus, if solving our housing crisis requires abandoning the idea that property is a vehicle for building wealth, perhaps it also means embracing the notion that creating valuable ideas or companies is the most noble thing a citizen can do.

This would require a complete inversion of our national outlook. Under the tyranny of tall poppy syndrome, it's as if property is the most excusable way to get rich in Australia: if you found a start-up, you're long on yourself; but if you invest in property, you're just long on Australia.

But we may not have a choice. For if pouring ever-larger piles of credit into unproductive assets is a sure-fire way of doing less with more, innovation has always meant doing more with less.

Joseph Walker

Correspondence

Judith Brett

In *The Great Divide*, Alan Kohler excavates two of the historical roots of the current housing crisis in the nineteenth century. The first was the abundance of land with low-density suburbs of free-standing dwellings sprawling further and further from the services of the CBD and little medium-density housing. This was turbo-charged in the 1950s, as car ownership grew and the suburbs spread out into farmland and market gardens – and they are still growing. The second is that land and property speculation was early established as an easy way to build wealth. This came crashing down in the 1890s when the land boom went bust, but Kohler argues that the treatment of housing as an investment asset was already well established.

This, though, was only ever for a small number of wealthy people. For most people, owning a home was primarily about having somewhere secure to live and raise a family, "one little piece of earth with a house and a garden which is ours; to which we can withdraw, in which we can be among our friends, into which no stranger may come against our will." This is Robert Menzies in 1943 in his radio broadcast to the Forgotten People, in which he used the home as an organising principle to enumerate the virtues of the Australian middle class. Menzies' broadcast is now widely seen as foreshadowing the boom in home ownership which started in the 1950s. But it also looked back, to the aspirations of the land-hungry British immigrants who poured into the Australian colonies during the nineteenth century and the importance of home ownership in building a stable society and a functioning democracy. Home ownership was not just about individual amenity but about building a nation. The current panic over housing affordability which threatens to price many young people out of ever owning a home is not just a panic about individual life options but about the sort of society Australia is becoming, about the weakening of social cohesion as inequality increases and we lose our sense of shared fate. To understand this, we also need to start with the nineteenth century.

Australia's post-war history has been so successfully periodised by journalism and popular history – particularly the decades of the 1950s and 1960s – that it can be hard to see more enduring patterns. The young couples forming their households and raising the baby boomers in the new post-war suburbs were fulfilling aspirations which had deep roots in Australia's experience: first of the land-hungry gold-rush immigrants, and then of the suburban nation which developed in the long boom from 1860 to 1890, in which the yeoman's longing for a plot of land and a cow was transformed into the aspiration for a home of one's own and a garden. And it was a remarkable feature of Australia that this aspiration could be more readily fulfilled here than anywhere else in the world at the time.

For the most part, this aspiration was fulfilled in the suburbs of Australia's capital cities. In comparison with crowded and expensive inner-city property, the suburbs offered affordable homes of one's own in healthy, peaceful, semi-rural surrounds. Decency, good order, health and domestic privacy were at the heart of the suburban ideal; and by the late nineteenth century the combination of high wages and cheap, easily serviced land had made suburban home ownership more affordable in Australia than in Britain or most parts of the United States. Graeme Davison estimates that in the early 1880s, 45.5 per cent of Melbourne households were owner occupiers, which was exceedingly high by contemporary world standards. With a different history and a geography less hospitable to easy development, Sydney's rate was lower, at 30 per cent. Observers were struck by the number of working men among the home-owners.

Home ownership quickly acquired political significance. The suburban ideology which developed during the land boom of the 1880s stressed the advantages of the settled life to woo restless immigrants from their wandering life and so build the white population. Property qualifications for voting had long linked the obligations of political citizenship to property ownership, and although the Australian colonies all had manhood suffrage for lower-house elections by the end of the nineteenth century, property qualifications remained for participation in upper-house and municipal elections. But the property qualifications, inherited from an England in which democratic rights were wrenched from the landed gentry and aristocracy, took on very different meanings in a settler society. In the new land of opportunity it was far more plausible to present property ownership as an indication of achievement and hence of the desirable citizenly qualities of independence, hard work and resourcefulness, than in the old world of hereditary wealth and social position. As well, property ownership became a sign of the property owner's commitment to the future of the colony, their building of "a stake in the country." The left has often interpreted the phrase "a stake in the country" to mean that property ownership was a conservative tool making one supportive of the status quo. But in a settler society like Australia, which needed people to settle – to commit their futures to the future of the colony and not to come, make a pile and go home again – the phrase had an additional layer of meaning. To build a house, a stake in the country, showed one intended to stay.

The depression of the 1890s ended Australia's first long boom, "the glad confident morning" in which boundless resources seemed to offer boundless opportunities to new immigrants, and to promise a society free from the miseries and fixed class divisions of the old world. As the depression struck, people's futures closed in and class divisions hardened. The failed great strikes of the 1890s and the formation of labour parties challenged colonial liberalism's optimistic, nation-building individualism with the politics of class. When the good times came again in the long post-war boom, aspirations for home ownership on hold since 1890 were able to be satisfied, overseen by Robert Menzies and the newly formed Liberal Party, to whom the links between home ownership, character, citizenship and nation were self-evident. The home was a key site in the formation of the strength of character on which good citizenship and the future of the nation depended. Home ownership was not just a private good, but a stable site from which one participated in the wider public world. The Australian dream was never just about individual aspiration. But that is what it has become, as housing has come to be seen as an asset rather than a place to live and its cost is eating up more and more of people's incomes.

Kohler graphically illustrates the divergence of house prices from income growth which began around 2000, and the wider impact this has had on the economy. Accompanying this has been an explosion of property investors, who see real estate as the surest way to build wealth – and not from rents but from price inflation. So as younger people have been priced out of home ownership, Australia has developed a rentier class, who are well represented in our parliaments. The halving of the capital gains tax by Howard's government accelerated property investment. Kohler judges that Howard did more than anyone to make housing unaffordable, quoting him that no one ever complained to him about increases in the values of their homes. These words of Howard's show that by the turn of the century home ownership was already losing its wider public and social meanings and becoming viewed primarily as an individual asset by the party that once saw it as the foundation of good citizenship.

But Howard was wrong to be so complacent. As Kohler shows, since 2000 the growth in house prices has so far outstripped wage growth that where once a house cost three to 3.5 times annualised average weekly earnings, it is now six to seven times and out of reach for increasing numbers of wage-earning Australians, unless they have access to family capital. Disconnecting work from realistic aspirations to home ownership is deeply corrosive of the values on which the Liberal Party was built: thrift, work, the desire for financial independence. And this is now evident in the way Kohler describes Australia as having had an egalitarian meritocracy. With talent and work, pretty well everyone who wanted to could buy a house. But now – why bother to work hard and save if you'll never get a house? And why vote conservative if you have nothing to conserve?

Judith Brett

Correspondence

Brendan Coates & Joey Moloney

Alan Kohler's *The Great Divide* is a compelling account of Australia's housing calamity and how it threatens to tear our society apart. Within living memory, Australia was a place where housing costs were manageable and people of all ages and incomes had a reasonable chance to own a home with good access to jobs. But the great Australian dream of home ownership is rapidly turning into a nightmare for many young Australians, while the growing divide between the housing "haves" and "have nots" risks returning Australia to the Jane Austen world of the late-eighteenth century.

Kohler correctly diagnoses the core driver of unaffordable housing: it's too hard to build more homes in established suburbs where people want to live. But having done so, he veers regrettably off-course to propose solutions that have little chance of working, and which simply act to distract his readers from the main game of building more homes. Kohler misses the moment. The political mood is changing. There is a growing groundswell of support for more density, and a growing awareness of the costs of locking up vast tracts of our cities from development. With momentum building and much more still to do, Kohler's misfire is particularly unfortunate.

Historically, Australia has not built enough housing to meet the needs of its growing population. Heading into the COVID-19 pandemic, Australia had just over 400 dwellings per 1000 people, which was among the least housing stock per person in the developed world. Australia had also experienced the second-greatest decline in housing stock relative to the adult population over the twenty years leading into COVID, and Australian cities are some of the least dense in the developed world.

The reason is simple. The frameworks and processes that dictate what gets built where are hugely biased against change. Older and wealthier residents of well-located suburbs – those who prefer their neighbourhoods to stay the same – get an outsized say. Prospective residents, who might live in new housing in desirable suburbs were it to be built, find themselves effectively unrepresented.

The result is "missing middles": hectares of prime inner-city land, close to jobs and transport, rising barely taller than two stories. The flow-on effect is high prices and rents, a stagnating economy because fewer people can live close to jobs, and expensive and environmentally damaging sprawl into farmland and floodplains.

If the problem is not enough homes in established suburbs, surely any meaningful solution must involve building more homes in said suburbs? But Kohler is unduly pessimistic, arguing that more medium-density housing is "going to be difficult, if not impossible," "won't work," and "will never actually happen."

Kohler contends that addressing the supply problem directly is too hard, and instead searches for alternatives that have little prospect of succeeding. He does this because he judges that the obvious answer – building more housing in the inner- and middle-ring suburbs of Australia's major cities where most Australians still want to live – is politically unworkable.

Kohler frames NIMBYism and heritage restrictions as "natural barriers" to greater density. But there's no natural law that says we must let the aesthetic preferences of existing residents for Victorian terraces or Californian bungalows trump the needs of their fellow Australians to have somewhere to live. The restrictive zones in desirable suburbs are not unalterable commandments handed down like ancient laws. Building denser cities is a political decision, and Kohler misses that the political tide is starting to turn.

Until recently, supply-side reform was an obsession for a passionate few, but largely absent from broader political discourse. But in recent times, the political clout of renters has grown and the YIMBY movement has gained momentum. Sacred cows are slowly being slaughtered. The Minns government in New South Wales has plans to up-zone large amounts of well-located land, including overriding heritage controls where they conflict with more density. Victoria is aiming to build 800,000 homes over the next decade, with at least 70 per cent in established suburbs. The Albanese government has put $3.5 billion of federal money on the table, mirroring a Grattan Institute recommendation, to push the states to help build 1.2 million homes over the next five years. This isn't just an Australian phenomenon. Similar shifts are taking place in the United States, Canada, the United Kingdom and New Zealand. Kohler has misread the political winds.

Key to this change is the fact that most residents of Sydney and Melbourne actually want more density if it means being able to live in a better-located suburb. Denser dwellings – townhouses, apartments, etc. – made up 44 per cent of Sydney's housing in 2016, and 33 per cent of Melbourne's. Yet a Grattan Institute survey showed that residents say they actually want those numbers to be 59 per cent in Sydney and 52 per cent in Melbourne.

The weight of evidence is becoming impossible to ignore. Take New Zealand: in 2016, Auckland – a city of 1.5 million – rezoned about three-quarters of its suburban area to allow more intensive land use. Researchers found that this led to a doubling of the city's rate of housing construction. Unsurprisingly, rents in Auckland are lower now – relative to inflation – than they were in 2016, whereas rents across the rest of New Zealand have gone up by 10 to 15 per cent over the same period.

Denser cities don't just offer cheaper housing. Done well, they also bring amenity, vibrancy and walkability; certainly, much more so than a satellite suburb fifty kilometres from the CBD. Several cities with similar populations but higher densities – such as Vancouver, Toronto and Vienna – outrank Sydney on quality-of-life measures.

But Kohler argues land-use planning reform is too hard, preferring an alternative approach: run faster trains to peri-urban and regional areas, massively increasing the commutable distance to our major cities. This would be unfair, costly and ineffective. Allowing more homes in desirable suburbs would enable more young Australians to live, work and add to the social fabric of these communities. Spending billions on trains from somewhere else tells them they're only wanted there for their labour, and the preferences of those who got there first matter more.

Denser cities are more efficient cities. The NSW Productivity Commission found it costs up to $750,000 less in infrastructure per home in established suburbs than on the urban fringe. Denser cities are also better for the climate – a sprawling, car-dependent city pumps more CO_2 into the atmosphere. And denser cities are better for the economy – allowing more employers to locate closer together increases knowledge spillovers and gives workers more options.

More fundamentally, fast trains simply would not solve the problem in the way Kohler contends they will. To be fast, trains need few stops, and few stops along low-density corridors means longer trips to the train station for commuters. Cutting fifteen minutes off a train ride from Geelong to Melbourne isn't much help if it's a forty-minute drive to the station, and a race against the clock to find a park before the train leaves. And at the other end, Kohler appears to believe most if not all workers need to get to the CBD. But Grattan research has found that only about 15 per cent of jobs are there, at least in Melbourne. So even after a trek to the station at one end, fast trains to the city still leave workers with more commuting to do at the other end.

The fast-trains solution would leave workers heavily exposed to one service that takes them a hundred kilometres from home. The denser-cities solution offers workers diversity and options. Some people will walk to work, some can ride their bike, others take the tram or train, and inevitably many will drive. But the key point is that when jobs are closer, it is easier for families to organise their lives – easier for one parent to pick up a sick toddler from daycare, or for the other to take a new job opportunity without upending family arrangements.

Australia's housing affordability crisis is needlessly compounded by muddled housing policy discourse. The heart of the problem is much simpler than many let on: housing costs are too high because there are not enough houses. Kohler provides an incisive critique of the political obstacles towards remedy. The political tide is starting to turn, but there is much more still to do. Distracting Australians with the superficial solution of building trains instead of houses is an unfortunate wrong turn.

Brendan Coates & Joey Moloney

Correspondence

Mark Walker

In *The Great Divide*, Alan Kohler correctly identifies a singular lack of mass public transportation, such as rail, as one of the reasons for the urban sprawl that blights our cities. He also questions why more of our regional centres have not developed as commuter cities, featuring more affordable housing, as is the case in Europe.

It is largely due to the well-known tyranny of distane that fewer rail lines were built either out of our major centres, or between secondary centres that were able to establish themselves regionally. Of those that were, many closed once motor transport became dominant, unable to compete with the speed and convenience of trucks and cars, which could utilise gearing and the grip of their rubber tyres to climb steep hills, whereas trains were limited to very gentle gradients due to the lack of grip between steel wheels and rails. This traction limitation required rail lines to closely follow the contours of the land, while budgetary constraints prevented them sweeping majestically across valleys on expensive viaducts, or ducking into even more expensive tunnels to avoid mountains, making them longer and more winding than is today ideal, and therefore much slower.

It is the convoluted, contour-following nature of the original nineteenth-century track alignment that still largely dictates the speed of trains today. To speed them up, we need to spend big on upgrading the actual line of rail – the embankments, viaducts and cuttings on which the rails are laid.

Why can we not simply purchase faster trains? The problem is centrifugal force. The faster a train travels, the gentler must be the bends in the track, or the engines and carriages can tip up, and tip over. Queensland Rail attempted to overcome this by using the famous "tilting trains" that use hydraulics to "tilt" the mass of the carriage towards the inside of the bend, thus enabling higher speeds and shorter travel times. But they are still limited to around 160 kilometres per hour, and only on a good day on a well-maintained track!

Very Fast Trains capable of 350 kilometres per hour, such as Japan's Shinkansen and France's TGV, require track with very low radius bends to achieve their much higher speeds. The track bed also needs to be utterly stable, which often requires specialist engineering, costly maintenance regimes or additional concrete reinforcing, especially in the acceleration and deceleration zones near stations.

Yet some countries have been able to establish a Fast Rail network that uses less expensive construction techniques and slightly slower rail stock. Spain, for example, with double our population yet only a tenth the area – with distances between major centres much shorter – has been able to develop Europe's longest Fast Train network (the Alta Velocidad Española, or AVE) comprising 3200 kilometres of its total 16,000 kilometres of rail, servicing all its major cities. Spain's AVE takes approximately three hours to travel the 450 kilometres between Madrid and Seville, equating to a six-hour trip between Sydney and Melbourne, using fully electric Fast Trains capable of 200 kilometres per hour. Had we similar Fast Trains – and straighter line of rail – here in Australia, it would be possible to commute from Sydney to Canberra, or Albury to Melbourne, in under two hours.

The other difficulty is that freight provides the main revenues for train line operators, not passengers, and the current thinking on this subject is to stick with diesel locomotives hauling double-decked freight wagons (as on the Melbourne to Brisbane Inland Rail Project). A continuing focus on this methodology could preclude electrification, as the upper container on a double-deck wagon would foul the gantries holding the power lines for the single-deck passenger and bulk-freight trains.

However, there is an argument for the electrification of inter-city rail, as part of our commitment to meeting carbon emission reduction targets, that could, eventually, lead to both cheaper and less polluting freight transportation, as well as faster passenger rail, and to the revitalisation of regional centres. Road freight accounts for 16 per cent of our overall carbon emissions. Rail, by contrast, produces only 4 per cent of total emissions, and this while utilising existing diesel-powered trains. Ideally, we should seek to electrify our rail network, reducing emissions to near zero, then move much of the road freight onto rail, to further reduce carbon emissions from transport, and making the rail lines more profitable.

If rail was electrified, especially with renewable energy drawn from regional renewable projects, it might also make sense – as a "nation-building" exercise – to straighten, realign and reconfigure our major inter-city train lines to enable the faster point-to-point times that would in turn enable regional centres to develop as commuter cities, as so many have in Europe.

The only previous serious attempt at decentralisation, noted by Kohler, was initiated by the Whitlam government fifty years ago. The resultant "growth centres" pioneered in the 1970s are today thriving regional hubs, largely self-supporting in terms of industry, employment and (relatively) affordable housing.

Perhaps it's time to revisit decentralisation – via rail realignment, electrification and implementation of Fast Trains? Such a policy would enable real population growth outside the major cities, putting downward pressure on housing costs nationally, while also achieving significant reduction of carbon emissions, enabling us to better and more quickly reach our emissions targets.

Mark Walker

Peter Tulip

Public discussion of housing policy suffers from undisciplined eclecticism. Too many commentators provide long, unstructured lists of multiple causes or conclude that the truth lies between competing explanations. This muddle reflects an inability or unwillingness to distinguish the important from the unimportant. Alan Kohler's *The Great Divide* and the accompanying media coverage are examples.

Instead, let's be clear. Housing costs are high and rising because growing demand interacts with unresponsive supply. This has been going on since at least the 1970s. Rising demand in turn reflects higher population, higher per-capita income and (since their peak in the 1980s) falling real mortgage rates. Taxes are not an important factor.

Unresponsive supply largely reflects zoning restrictions. If the housing market worked like other consumer goods markets, higher demand would have resulted in many more dwellings. Instead, restricted supply has resulted in soaring prices.

Alan Kohler gets much of this right. His analysis of the dimensions of the problem and how it is ripping the social fabric apart is readable and incisive. And his discussion of zoning restrictions is spot-on. As he notes, zoning is estimated to have raised the price of housing in our biggest cities by hundreds of thousands of dollars. Those estimates are in line with an enormous body of research. (Full disclosure: Kohler cites my research on zoning approvingly.)

Kohler covers a wide range of other issues. I confine my comments to my biggest concern: his overemphasis of tax concessions. He argues that the interaction of negative gearing with discounted capital gains taxes is a major reason housing is unaffordable.

There is no credible research supporting this claim. On the contrary, good researchers have estimated the effect of negative gearing and capital gains tax concessions on housing prices using different approaches and repeatedly found this effect to be tiny. John Daley and Danielle Wood compared the revenue cost of the concessional treatment of capital gains tax and negative gearing to the value of the housing stock – and on that basis estimated that the tax concessions may boost the level of housing prices by 1 to 2.2 per cent. Gene Tunny, using a similar methodology and assumptions as Daley and Wood, found larger impacts of up to 4 per cent on house prices on average. The most detailed study is by Yunho Cho, Shuyun May Li and Lawrence Uren. In a micro-founded model, they found that removing negative gearing would reduce house prices by 0.9 per cent and raise rents 2.5 per cent. Deloitte Access Economics estimated the ALP's 2019 policy of restricting negative gearing to new housing and reducing the capital gains discount would reduce established dwelling prices by 4.6 per cent and new dwelling prices by 3.6 per cent. Effects of only eliminating negative gearing would be smaller.

In summary, negative gearing and the capital gains discount are estimated to boost house prices between 1 and 4 per cent, while having a smaller negative effect on rents. Most of these estimates represent a long-run "one-off" effect that would have been incorporated into housing prices decades ago.

It does not require technical research to see that the tax concessions are unimportant. Kohler points to the acceleration in prices after capital gains were discounted in 1999. However, the logic of that argument would imply that prices

Real residential property prices

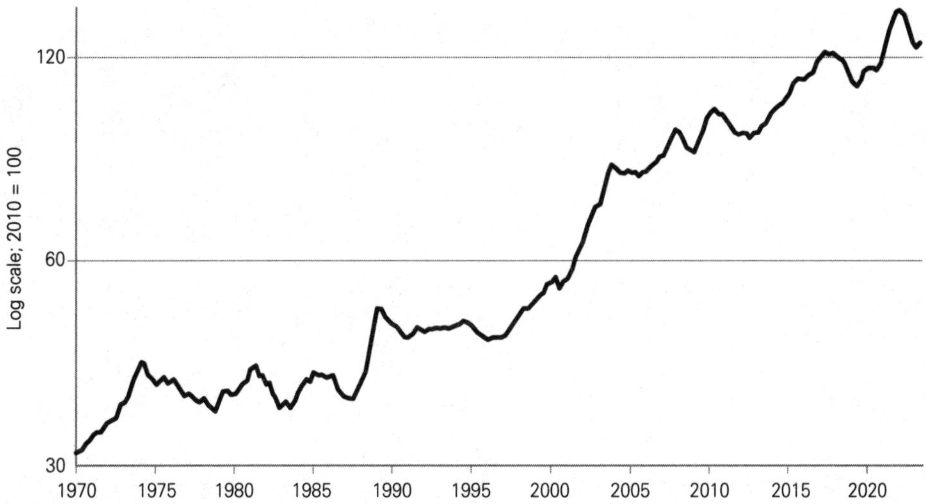

Source: St Louis Fed (FRED) database; series QAUR628BI

should have fallen by twice as much following the introduction of capital gains tax in 1985. Instead, prices rose. Taxes on investor housing were much lower in the early 1980s but prices were lower.

The evidence Kohler provides for a large effect of the tax concessions is a chart showing housing prices accelerated after 1999. That chart uses an arithmetic scale, which exaggerates the change. If instead one plots house prices on a log scale – as is standard for variables subject to exponential growth – an acceleration can be seen, but it is not dramatic and it begins before the tax change.

Empirical studies of housing prices, such as my 2019 paper with Trent Saunders or more recent work by Peter Abelson and Roselyne Joyeux, attribute the faster recent growth to lower real mortgage rates and higher immigration. They give no role to tax concessions.

The fundamental problem underlying the housing crisis is that voters oppose more housing in their neighbourhood because they don't know – or don't care – about the harm this opposition does. That needs to be explained to them. Kohler's discussion of zoning restrictions and their effect on Australian society is very good in this respect. However, public education also requires paying attention to the research and not being distracted by unimportant side issues.

Peter Tulip

Nicholas Reece

Alan Kohler's Quarterly Essay, *The Great Divide*, makes an important contribution to the hotly debated issue of Australia's housing mess. In an erudite and entertaining style, Alan navigates the history of policymaking and politicking that has led Australia, of *all* countries, to have a shortage of houses.

Alan's analysis is at its best when exploring the economic drivers of the housing crisis and the role of the taxation system and misguided government grants programs. However, his analysis of the planning system and the critique of state and local government misses some key points and requires a response.

For the last six years, I have served as a councillor and deputy lord mayor at the City of Melbourne and observed closely the way the planning system, local politics and developer activity impacts on the housing market.

The "simple lie" being told is that the housing mess is caused by local councils pandering to NIMBYs by not approving new residential development. The "complex truth" is that many other factors cause the housing supply shortage.

Most local governments in Australia assess planning applications within the statutory time limits and are pulling their weight when it comes to approving new residential development. A recent study by SGS Economics found that, on average, the planning system in Victoria approved about 38,000 multi-unit dwellings for development statewide – more than enough to meet demand. Further analysis by the Municipal Association of Victoria shows planning permits have been approved for 120,000 dwellings, but construction has not commenced.

In the City of Melbourne, I often describe us as a YIMBY council. There are currently well over 100 residential development projects with 22,000 dwellings for which we have given planning approval but which have not commenced. This is the equivalent of half of all the new homes Victoria needs in the next year in one municipality.

Poor, politicised or dodgy planning decisions rightly receive a lot of scrutiny and criticism. There is certainly scope for improvement in planning processes. But that should not take away from the fact that councils effectively facilitate massive amounts of development every year. And they do this with high levels of community input embedded in the process. That community involvement is in turn an important factor in maintaining confidence in the system. I happen to think it also leads to better decisions, at least most of the time.

This highlights the real and complex causes of the problem. As Alan says so succinctly, in Australia "governments don't build houses, developers do." And developers will only build projects where they are confident they can make a dollar. In the current market, developers are not starting construction because building and materials costs are sky-high, interest rates are up, insurance costs are soaring, and a spate of building company closures is creating project risk. State governments around Australia have also embarked on a record-breaking infrastructure spend. To be fair, much of this is catch-up after decades of underspend. But they are trying to squeeze a thirty-year pipeline of new infrastructure into ten years. The result is major skills and labour shortages for the residential building sector and overheated construction costs. When developers run the numbers over a new residential project in Australia, they just can't make it stack up. As a result, Australia is suffering from historic lows in new dwelling commencements, right at the time when demand is high and new supply is needed most.

Kohler also turns his analysis to the vexed issue of land supply and the locating of new residential development with good amenity, especially transport links to employment centres. He writes that "significantly increasing the density of housing within 10 to 30 kilometres of Australia's CBDs – which is what is required – is going to be difficult, if not impossible."

This overlooks the fact that most Australian capital cities have significant "growth areas" that exist relatively close to the CBD or along major transport corridors. Due to the good work of city planners in earlier times, Australia's capital cities are blessed with large tracts of land that have been used for industrial, port, aviation, rail and other uses. These areas could be converted into medium- to high-density residential and mixed-use areas for millions of Australians.

In recent decades we have seen the conversion of old industrial areas into new residential suburbs, such as Docklands in Melbourne and Green Square in Sydney. In Melbourne alone, old industrial areas such as Fishermans Bend, Lorimer, Arden and Macaulay have been designated as "renewal areas" which will be transformed into residential and employment precincts. Add to this Port Melbourne, Footscray, Cremorne and in future years Dynon and Docklands (E-Gate), as well as former industrial areas in Brunswick, Preston and Coburg and other inner and middle suburbs. These areas could house up to 1 million extra people.

A second major opportunity is available along existing train and tram lines and, in some instances, even major arterial roads where there is a first-rate bus service. Rezoning of height and density limits along these transport corridors will provide the opportunity for large numbers of people to live in good locations that are well serviced by transport. The precincts around major railway stations within the existing rail network provide the perfect location for these new medium-density suburbs. Tram corridors close to the city also are well positioned to accommodate more residents along their routes. In Melbourne alone, another 1 million people could be accommodated in these "transport growth corridors" within the existing metropolitan boundaries.

Alan Kohler also flags the brave and sensible idea of utilising the land assembly powers by state and local government. Converting many low-density suburbs to moderate medium-density is hard. Currently we are seeing scores of large single suburban blocks being converted into rows of units with a gun-barrel driveway. Robin Boyd would be turning in his grave at this latest addition to the Australian Ugliness. From a design perspective, the outcome is hideous. Land assembly can help overcome this problem by aggregating multiple blocks, which can then be master planned and developed to deliver high-quality, well-designed medium-density housing. The land assembly activity should be focused on areas close to railway stations and transport hubs. The politics of land assembly is obviously challenging. But in recent times, state governments have proven to be very brave and very good at undertaking land assembly activities when delivering major new transport projects and hospitals. It is time to turn this activity to housing.

A final small but important idea. New design rules and thinking for housing could also deliver improved affordability. For example, apartments built for the investor market have a bathroom for every bedroom. But this is not needed for apartments where people are planning to live long-term. Design rules could also make better use of communal spaces, delivering smaller and more affordable apartments that have larger communal areas and features such as a shared laundry on each floor. Through clever design thinking we can cut the cost of housing construction while still delivering high-quality homes.

Nicholas Reece

Correspondence

Pete Wargent

Alan Kohler's Quarterly Essay, *The Great Divide*, challenges the assumption that Australians actually want to fix housing affordability and supply, given that a quiet majority arguably hold a vested interest in the status quo. Assuming we genuinely want to bring about changes which promote both home ownership and housing affordability, I argue that this should be tackled in the form of a regional renaissance.

Australia's biennial intergenerational reports regularly prosecute the case for swelling the resident population to 40 million and beyond through ongoing net immigration. We're on a course which, if pursued, realistically means that affordable homes in landlocked Enmore or Erskineville simply won't be achievable. Logically, a change of focus is therefore required. The COVID-19 pandemic unexpectedly presented a remarkable window for employees to demonstrate the ability to work productively and flexibly from home, or closer to home. We should embrace this opportunity to create a broader vision for dynamic regional living.

Of course, economists will justifiably argue that the major capital cities have certain unique benefits in terms of economies of scale, concentration of skills, frequency of interactions, and the potential for serendipitous events. This is all incontestably true. But instead of trying solely to work out how we can cram twenty million people into Sydney, Melbourne and south-east Queensland's narrow coastal strip, perhaps we should create a grander and more enlightened vision for dynamic and thriving regional cities?

Let's start with, say, Albury-Wodonga, Bathurst, Dubbo, Orange, Port Macquarie and Wagga Wagga in New South Wales, as well as Ballarat, Bendigo, Mildura and Shepparton in Victoria. In Queensland we have Bundaberg, Cairns, Gladstone, Mackay and Rockhampton, for example, and in Western Australia Albany, Bunbury, Busselton and Geraldton. Add in Tasmania's Launceston, plus the already-popular peri-urban conurbations within a two-hour sweep of the larger capital cities, and here we have several dozen regional cities and centres which can be the thrust and heartbeat of a dynamic, productive and prosperous Aussie economy. Where people can have space, quality of life and affordable housing.

Australia has been accused in the past of being lucky and lazy, of running faceless and fattened oligopolies, of enjoying the fortune of vast mineral resources, while being a relatively favoured destination for global capital and wealth. The *Mittelstand* economies of Germany, Austria and Switzerland have variously demonstrated how we may be able to promote geographical diversity, driven forward by growth in nimble and adaptive small-to-medium enterprise (SME) businesses with a global niche, and a focus on technology and excellence. The edge in SME businesses over the big end of town can be in faster decision-making and elite customer service, offering a more human experience.

Life can be challenging for small businesses in a high-cost economy, with *Mittelstand* economies sometimes encouraging cooperatives or partnerships. SME businesses can excel by doing one thing really well, while working collaboratively with innovative technologies and AI to deliver innovation, entrepreneurship, outstanding training and apprenticeships, and quality customer experiences, with strong regional ties. Craft trades, machinery, electronics, chemicals, automotive parts and a raft of services industries can all fit the bill for growth.

More years ago than I would like to remember, I had some experience of living in Germany when I studied there in the *Oberstufe*. Germany has had its own housing market and other challenges in recent years, fuelled in part by shifting migration trends and in particular a dozen years of ultra-low interest rates, although house prices notched a record decline in 2023.

My best memories of Stuttgart – today a safe and flourishing city of 600,000 people with its vast sporting stadium, outstanding universities and growing start-up culture – might broadly fit the vision. You can live in the hills five or six kilometres from the heart of the city, with suburbs and villages populated by small business owners and workers in sectors ranging from engineering to personal services. Granted, home ownership rates are not high in Germany. Tenant-friendlier markets lead many to actively opt for long-term leases, enjoying an outstanding quality of life, while taking pride in business expertise and excellence. There could be something worthwhile to learn from this.

There may also prove to be some productivity challenges associated with more Aussies working from home (or perhaps closer to home, in serviced office hubs and not always in the central business districts). Many of the key market players in realty have a material stake in the large commercial office towers, but ultimately floor space will fill up over time, given the projections for population growth.

In Australia, our respective levels of government will need to invest in regional infrastructure – perhaps funded via land value capture – including in transport, educational facilities and healthcare. Why can't we live in Townsville or Toowoomba instead of cramming into Brisbane's northside mortgage belt? We'd need to see more appealing employment options and shopping hubs; high-speed internet and connectivity; great schools; road, rail and airports; healthcare excellence; leisure; and attractive housing choices. We need to create a vison, buzz and excitement, and a sense that "Hey, something is really happening here."

Incentives such as tax breaks and special economic zones can bring all the usual political challenges associated with the picking of winners, but why can't the Gold Coast be our regional technology hub, with Adelaide specialising in healthcare R&D, and, say, the Pilbara firing up as a leading renewable energy region? Australia is set to experience an array of booming industries ahead, including in green energy and energy security, niche manufacturing, food, healthcare R&D, construction techniques, mining, IT and other modern technologies besides.

Immigration and labour market settings are hotly contested, especially following the snap-back in arrivals as the international borders reopened, but there should clearly be a focus on upskilling the incumbent population, as well as importing more people. In professional services, it has for too long been the case that managers and directors are often imported rather than homegrown. More apprenticeships and vocational training would be a welcome reform, with higher education teaching our required skills and vocations, and not functioning so much as visa factories for international students.

Zoning reform in the capital cities has a key role to play in the housing conundrum; but equally rezoning doesn't fix everything. I recall living close to Newstead, in inner Brisbane, around a decade ago as a vast swathe of apartment towers began to mushroom out of the ground. The large oversupply of Brisbane apartments was even called out in the Reserve Bank of Australia's Financial Stability Review as a systemic risk for the economy. The idea that only half a dozen years down the track we would be debating the need for rezoning due to there not being enough development sites would have seemed absurd at the time.

What happened? Concerned consumers stopped buying new apartments, developers put up the shutters and sold off their surplus development sites, and as advertised rents declined the vacancies gradually filled up. Today we are back in a shortage, but by 2026 or 2027 that will quite likely have reverted to a supply overhang. No doubt there could be short-term uplift from rezoning, and overall it would be beneficial to housing supply over time. But over the long run supply and demand tends to revert towards equilibrium, so rezoning is one part of the housing solution, not the miracle cure.

A contemporary example to illustrate the point might be Hamilton Northshore in Brisbane, which can potentially absorb up to 25,000 people in 14,000 apartments, being a large, flat strip of land, effectively ready for development. Why has this supply not all built through the past cycle? Because the cycle was killed by oversupply, high vacancy rates, sliding prices and presales drying up.

There is little speculative building in Australia, and generally speaking new housing will only be built when it is profitable and viable to do so. House prices reflect both demand and supply, and the equilibrium price will occur at the level that matches current demand to available supply. In the short run, supply is increasingly relatively inelastic, given that we have more medium-density construction in the capital cities these days, and that it can take several years to bring new apartment projects to market.

Fixing the rental market is another challenge to be overcome. Tenants' rights have improved, but the other side of that coin is that there is less protection for landlords than there once was. Many private landlords would doubtless like to offer longer-term leases, but since it's sometimes difficult to evict even the most problematic of tenants, we are likely stuck with six- or twelve-month leases as things stand.

The burgeoning build to rent (BTR) sector can be a part of the housing solution for the capital cities, but it is also not the whole solution. The UK experience, centred in London, has been mixed. Total returns for the sector over the past half-decade have been modest rather than compelling, even including capital growth. If we take the risk-free rate to be the ten-year bond yield, this has been tracking at around 4 per cent. In Australia we have been assessing BTR portfolios on compressed cap rates of around only 4 to 5 per cent. Will the BTR sector deliver affordable rents? It's doubtful, given the institutional imperative and the required returns.

Overall, there are numerous challenges ahead for Australian housing market dynamics, dwelling supply and affordability. But with a relative shift in focus from the metropolitan melee to a regional renaissance, they needn't be insurmountable. We've seen a rush to the regions during the pandemic "race for space." Next, we need to champion a regional powerhouse campaign. The time to plan and invest is now!

Pete Wargent

Correspondence

Peter Mares

In his engaging, avuncular style, Alan Kohler lays out the drivers of Australia's housing mess with admirable clarity and emphasises its profound implications for inequality and social mobility. I have already sung the praises of *The Great Divide* in a review for *Inside Story*. Here, I want to pick at one of the knots Kohler identifies: the challenge of "the missing middle."

This phrase refers to the lack of medium-density dwellings – three- to four-storey apartment buildings that could offer a midpoint between the high-rise residential towers sprouting up in our city centres and the detached houses that continue their outward march on the urban fringes.

The concept of the missing middle can also be applied geographically to indicate the lack of significant new construction in middle-ring suburbs. This is evident in the Albanese government's desire to see 1.2 million "well-located" new homes built over five years, where "well-located" is code for close to shops, transport, jobs and services. In other words, the federal government wants new homes to be constructed in established suburbs and to utilise existing infrastructure. Yet urban infill is easier said than done. The roots of the challenge lie in the fragmented pattern of land ownership set in place as our cities grew.

As Kohler writes, in the post-war decades, our cities spread rapidly outwards from their dense nineteenth-century centres as the combination of affordable cars, near full employment, mass migration and available land induced families to build freestanding homes on large plots. The great Australian dream was born and locked in a sprawling urban form that is resistant to change. Once you've constructed neighbourhoods this way, asks demographer Simon Kuestenmacher, "how do you add medium density?"

Kuestenmacher's crucial question takes Kohler to "the problem of state and local governments and their control of housing supply through zoning."

There is no doubt that planning and zoning regulations can be a barrier to building denser housing in established neighbourhoods. Principle 4 of the Brisbane City Council's "Future Blueprint" is "protect our backyard," yet the Queensland government's vision for shaping south-east Queensland foresees that 94 per cent of Brisbane's additional housing will come from "consolidation" within the city's existing urban boundary rather than from "expansion" beyond it. The contradiction between these two objectives set by two different levels of government is glaring.

The problem is not confined to the Sunshine State. The aspiration in Plan Melbourne is for 70 per cent of new housing to 2050 to be constructed in established suburbs and just 30 per cent in expanding greenfield developments on the metropolitan fringe. Other capital cities have similarly ambitious targets for urban consolidation, and, like Melbourne, most are falling well short of meeting them.

There are inevitable tensions between local-level decision-making and an overarching metropolitan strategy. Existing residents can reasonably expect to have a say in the future shape of their neighbourhoods and to resist their leafy greenness being steamrolled to meet state planning targets. Yet hyper-localism can also thwart the rational reorganisation of our cities to accommodate growing populations, adapt to a changing climate and contribute to a low-emissions economy.

The conventional response to the pressing problem of the missing middle is to identify planning and zoning as barriers to building more homes, and to see their removal as the pre-eminent solution. The property industry consistently argues that deregulation is the answer to our housing woes because it will free up the market, allowing developers to increase supply and bring down prices. Yet as Kohler points out, developers only build when they can make a profit. In November 2016, a seventy-storey tower with a hotel and 488 apartments was approved on the block adjacent to my apartment in Melbourne's CBD. Seven years later the only "development" has been that the site was sold for a massive capital gain. The City of Melbourne endorsed the new owner's revised plans, and construction was supposed to commence in 2022. There's still no sign of any work. Meanwhile, a five-storey building sits empty.

Planning constraints may inhibit construction, but their removal does not automatically prompt building. The longstanding quest to unlock residential development by streamlining regulation has so far generated meagre returns, with significant reforms to planning regimes making no appreciable dent on real estate prices. The response is to double down: if housing is too expensive, then that means there's not enough housing being built, so our deregulation efforts are insufficient and we must deregulate even more. This relentless focus on housing *supply* blends out any discussion of housing *distribution* and distracts from other core issues like tax settings.

Still, planning reform now looks set to ramp up another notch as state governments threaten to override more local council powers and amend planning regimes. In future, proposals to replace free-standing family homes with rows of townhouses or to build granny flats to backyards are likely to get swifter, simplified approvals. While this will increase density, such piecemeal infill is likely to erode the amenity of established suburbs, without providing either the scale or quality of housing we need.

In October, at a webinar run by SGS Economics & Planning, SGS principal and partner Patrick Fensham argued that achieving a 70/30 split of new housing between existing suburbs and greenfield projects means building 600 to 700 dwellings *per week* within current urban boundaries. To date, where this type of residential construction has occurred, he says, it's mostly taken two forms. First, there's the conversion of former industrial land into housing – Melbourne's Docklands is an example – but opportunities to redevelop such "brownfield" sites are becoming scarce. Second, there is residential intensification around "activity centres," particularly major transport hubs and shopping centres. Melbourne's Box Hill and Sydney's Ashfield are examples, though, as Fensham says, these are high-rise clusters, not medium-density housing.

The opportunity yet to be grasped lies in the "greyfields" – the freestanding family homes and backyards of middle suburbia. Much of this housing is reaching its use-by date in terms of energy efficiency, thermal comfort and maintenance costs. It was designed in an era when a family with two or more kids was the dominant demographic typology. Today, with smaller families, and more single and couple-only households, we need different dwelling types. Fensham argues that the old suburban lot must be the building block for the future. It is on these "greyfields" that new, denser, greener and more affordable housing can be constructed. Yet this poses a fundamental challenge, because a single suburban lot is too small to accommodate the quality, midrise housing that constitutes the missing middle. If we are going to meet our 70/30 aspirations, we need first to overcome the fragmented pattern of land ownership established in post-war subdivisions.

In *The Art of the Engine Driver*, the first of his award-winning Glenroy series, novelist Steven Carroll chronicles family life on Melbourne's edge in the 1950s as new suburbs were stamped out of farmland. Today Glenroy is middle ring and ripe for redevelopment – in fact, despite planning and zoning constraints, ad hoc redevelopment is already happening. In his webinar presentation, SGS's Fensham used Glenroy to provide a compelling illustration of how established neighbourhoods might be reimagined, and the opportunity that will be lost if we continue our present trajectory.

Fensham took a sample block of twenty-six lots bounded by four streets. The original subdivision was characterised by detached houses with big backyards. Less than 20 per cent of the land was covered by buildings, an extensive tree canopy cooled the landscape and deep soils absorbed the rain. A first phase of redevelopment saw some of these freestanding houses replaced by single-level semi-detached villa units, two or three to a lot. Next came double-storey semi-detached townhouses, and more recently, rows of double-storey attached townhouses, with as many as five dwellings squeezed onto a parcel of land. If business continues as usual, then before long the block's original twenty-six houses will have been replaced by ninety-one dwellings. This would constitute a significant increase in density, but at the cost of almost all tree cover and with the old backyards given over to buildings. What little open space remains will generally be buried under concrete.

Fensham offers an alternative vision for coordinated redevelopment in which those twenty-six separate lots are amalgamated into larger parcels of land to enable the construction of 165 European-style medium-density dwellings. This would achieve much greater housing density than piecemeal infill, yet the building footprint would only take up about 40 per cent of the total land area, leaving plenty of open space for pocket parks, gardens and trees.

It is a much more appealing prospect for suburbia than the hot, hard, unforgiving landscape that will result from the business-as-usual approach to urban consolidation, in which houses are knocked down and replaced one by one. But achieving a denser, greener future will require, in Fensham's words, "a much more interventionist role" for the public sector to assemble land, master-plan sites and, potentially, constrain developments that won't achieve the desired densities or which would destroy the existing amenity of trees and open space.

So our key housing challenge is not to get government out of the way so business can get on with rebuilding middle-ring suburbs; it is for government to more actively assist developers to amalgamate sites and reconfigure entire precincts, while engaging with residents to allay their fears and realise their aspirations.

Planning should not be the barrier to building the housing we need, but the enabler.

Peter Mares

Correspondence

Saul Eslake

Just over ten years ago, I gave a talk to a dinner organised by the Henry George League (a small but enthusiastic group dedicated to the ideas promulgated by Henry George, a nineteenth-century economist and journalist best remembered today for his advocacy of a "single tax" on the unimproved value of land), which three months later formed the basis for a submission I provided to a Senate committee enquiry into affordable housing. Both were titled "Australian Housing Policy: Fifty Years of Failure." If I were to give the same talk again – or write a similar submission to yet another parliamentary inquiry – the only things I would change would be to update the numbers I quoted in it and change the title from "Fifty Years of Failure" to "Sixty Years of Failure." Because that's what the policies of governments of all political persuasions, at all three levels – federal, state or territory, and local – have been. An unmitigated failure.

Alan Kohler was kind enough to quote from that talk in his Quarterly Essay. Indeed, Kohler went much further back into history than I did – to the mid-1820s. After reading his essay, I could almost speak of Australian housing policy as entailing 200 years of failure – except for the three decades or so after World War II when, as Kohler documented, Australian housing policy did succeed in meeting its stated goals of increasing home ownership and providing an adequate stock of affordable rental housing for those unable to attain home ownership.

To my way of thinking, one of the valuable contributions which Kohler's essay makes to the contemporary debate about Australia's housing crisis is in drawing out the history which shows that governments can – if they make the "right" policy choices – ensure that people can afford to buy or rent a home, even when faced with more rapid growth in the population (and hence in the "underlying" demand for housing) than we have experienced over the past eighteen months.

That is what they did between the end of World War II and the mid-1960s, when Australia's population grew at an average annual rate of 2.2 per cent per annum (compared with 1.6 per cent per annum over the past twenty years), and the population of Australia's eight capital cities grew at an average annual rate of 3.4 per cent per annum (because, in addition to the postwar "baby boom" and the massive immigration program, Australians were also moving from rural areas to state capitals in large numbers). Yet despite that, the average price of housing remained unchanged, as a multiple of average earnings, at about 3.5 times: and the home ownership rate rose by 20 percentage points – from 52.5 per cent to 72.5 per cent – between the 1947 and 1966 censuses.

That was possible because governments of both political persuasions, at both the federal and state levels, as well as local governments, focused on expanding the supply of housing and, beyond the bipartisan support for a big immigration program, refrained from adding to the demand for housing. Yes, as Kohler points out, there were ideological differences between the two major parties as to whether public housing should be sold to prospective buyers. But there was a bipartisan commitment to ensuring that the supply of housing matched the demand for it.

As Kohler goes on to show, that commitment began to waver, beginning with the introduction of the first program of cash grants to would-be first home buyers by the Menzies government in 1964. I don't think it's a coincidence that the home ownership rate peaked at the first census after that and has been declining ever since. At the federal and state levels, governments of both political persuasions have increasingly favoured policies which have the effect of inflating the demand for housing; while at the state and local level, governments have increasingly favoured policies which have the effect of adding to the cost or the difficulty (or both) of increasing the supply of housing.

In my view, history amply demonstrates that anything which allows Australians to pay more for housing than they otherwise would – be it cash grants to first-time buyers, stamp duty concessions for first-time buyers, preferential tax treatment for residential property investors, government guarantees for loans to people who have difficulty accumulating the required deposit, shared equity schemes, lower interest rates, or easier standards for determining loan eligibility – results in Australians paying more for housing, and hence higher housing prices, rather than in higher home ownership rates.

Yet, despite the accumulation of six decades' worth of history amply demonstrating that point, governments of all political persuasions keep doing the same things – and, echoing Albert Einstein's definition of insanity – expecting a different result.

Another of Kohler's valuable contributions is to point out why. As he says, "housing is a cartel of the majority, with the banks and the developers helping them maintain high house prices with the political class actively supporting them. Everybody involved in this game – home owners, banks, developers and state and federal politicians – wants house prices to rise for their own reasons."

I'd put the same point slightly differently. Over the past thirty years, there have been, on average, about 112,000 first home buyers in any given year. Up until the moment they sign their purchase contracts and draw down their mortgages, they (presumably) want governments to do things that would restrain the rate of increase in property prices. But at any point in time, there are more than 6.2 million households – which probably means at least 10 million individuals (out of 17.7 million on the electoral roll) – who own (individually or with a spouse or partner) the dwelling in which they live – all of whom have a vested interest in governments doing things that boost the rate of increase in property prices.

One thing that successful politicians can do is to count votes. And they know that there are far more votes to be had from people who want property prices to keep going up than there are from people who want them to stop going up, or even to go down. And that, I've come to believe, is the real reason why what Kohler calls "Australia's housing mess" will probably never be cleaned up by government policies: because a majority of voters don't want it to be cleaned up. And politicians know that.

Saul Eslake

Stephen Smith

Alan Kohler's essay is an excellent summary of the key issues which have contributed to Australia's housing affordability crisis. It is one of the few substantial, lucid analyses to comprehensively consider the contribution of poor policy to both insufficient housing supply and excessive housing demand.

Alan aims most of his rhetorical barbs at the political class – of all persuasions, and all three levels of government, over many decades. In Alan's narrative, politicians are the primary perpetrators of the problem, as well as the custodians of the solutions.

Politicians do indeed carry a significant share of the responsibility. Alan expertly sets out the perverse political incentives which have discouraged policy change in areas such as tax, land release, zoning and public housing that would have helped to correct (or at least not exacerbate) the crisis. In this area of policy, politicians have had little reason to prioritise all of society at the expense of existing home owners.

But politicians are not wholly responsible. If they were, Australia's housing pain would be a global anomaly. In some ways it is – Alan makes the point that each country's experience is unique. But the unaffordability of decent, well-located housing for people of average means is an issue for many countries around the world. And housing is not the only asset class which has become "unaffordable" when using Alan's preferred metric of price growth consistently and substantially outpacing income growth. From commercial property, infrastructure and the share market to art, wine and vintage cars, the prices of investable assets around the world have exploded over the past few decades. So much so that the phenomenon has in recent years been described as an "everything bubble."

Why has that happened? It is worth stepping back for a moment to consider how an asset is priced. In financial markets, and with some simplification, the value of an asset is equal to the amount of income it can generate over time. For residential property, that income is the rent paid to the landlord (or the rent that would be paid, for property owned by the occupier). So, setting aside complications such as tax and other expenses, the value of a residential property should be equal to the total amount of rent it can provide the owner from now into perpetuity.

That sounds straightforward enough. But a dollar of rent today is not the same as a dollar of rent tomorrow. Or next year. Or next decade. To be compared with today's dollars, future rent needs to be "discounted." What discount rate should be used? Again, setting aside some complications, one relevant benchmark would be the risk-free interest rate, typically considered to be the interest rate on ten-year government debt.

That's critical, because interest rates (on ten-year government debt, and more generally) have spent the last four decades charting a slow but steady course downwards towards zero. By definition, that downward trend in interest rates has caused the value or price of all assets – including residential property – to be regularly and consistently revised upwards.

The past four decades were special. A number of factors combined to put downward pressure on interest rates: demographic change, the rapid growth of China and other emerging economies with relatively high savings rates, more globally interconnected financial markets and a vast increase in international capital flows, technological change and more complex financial products. As a result, debt ballooned. In the 1970s, the world had borrowed $1.15 of debt for every $1 of economic activity. By 2022, that ratio had more than doubled, with the world having accumulated $2.38 of debt for every $1 of economic activity.

This is the "financialisation" of the economy that Alan makes several brief references to in his essay, but with little elaboration about how this has contributed to the housing crisis. Housing is a unique class of asset. As Alan notes several times, housing should be seen as a basic human right and not a source of wealth creation. Unfortunately, that ship sailed long ago.

What might come next? Interest rates temporarily reached zero during the pandemic. They may not rise substantially from here, but nor is there much room left for interest rates to continue to fall. That does not mean the "everything bubble" will burst. But it will inflate with less enthusiasm in the years ahead, giving average incomes time to make up some ground on house prices.

Ultimately, this is all a matter of timing. Good timing, or bad, depending on your perspective and, quite likely, your age. The issue is not so much that millennials and gen Zs have been dealt a bad hand. Rather, it is that baby boomers (and many gen Xers) won the generational lottery. That may appear to be a false distinction. The point is that the baby boomers are the first, and very likely the only, generation in which an individual of average means can retire wealthy – perhaps even a multi-millionaire – solely on the basis of having owned their own home. That wasn't possible for any previous generation, and it probably won't be possible for any future generation.

Just like a surprised lottery winner at the local newsagent, older generations don't need to feel guilty. But they should at least recognise their good fortune and be willing to share the windfall profits they have accumulated via the tax system. Otherwise, the risk that existing intergenerational inequality morphs into a broader schism in Australian society, as Alan alludes to, is very real.

With interest rates no longer on a downward trend, their contribution to any further inflating of Australian property prices will be muted at most. That means that while politicians are not wholly responsible for the problem, they are wholly responsible for the remaining solutions.

No wonder Alan ends his essay on a pessimistic note. It's hard to feel anything but.

Stephen Smith

THE GREAT DIVIDE

Correspondence

Evan Thornley & Jane-Frances Kelly

Housing is an enormously complex subject, frequently misunderstood by experts and the public alike. Alan Kohler's insightful analysis navigates through the historical evolution and policy complexities, rightly diagnosing that our challenges have been decades in the making. He is astute in his observation that it's difficult for governments to act, as housing policy change generally creates losers as well as winners (in any given year, the number of home owners with an interest in high house prices is vastly larger than those trying to get into the market).

But the view that if only governments could muster the political courage to alter some policy settings, this could all be fixed is, sadly, wrong. We wish it were that easy.

The role of government incentives and interest rates can be overstated in their effect on house prices. Over the last twenty years, house prices have grown on average by just over 7 per cent a year, a $7.1 trillion increase. Government policy, in the form of preferential tax treatment and incentives for property assets, is often asserted as the main reason for this growth. However, the Reserve Bank of Australia has published estimates that the capital gains tax exemption and negative gearing combined account for less than 2 per cent of the multi-trillion-dollar recent growth in house prices.

Meanwhile, media commentary typically focuses on the role of interest rates. But property prices increased substantially during the thirty years of rising interest rates after World War II, as well as in thirty years of falling rates after 1990 (and as rates have increased more recently). While both interest rates and tax policies are relevant, they don't explain most of the growth we've seen in Australia over many decades.

So, what is the biggest driver of the growth of house prices over such a long period? We think the single largest thing that is underplayed is the importance of land value.

Land has a significant and outsized role in house prices because it's not like other things we buy. We all need a place to live, so land is different from the kinds of goods where, if the price gets too high, people can opt out of using it (hence, if necessary, people stop eating out in order to continue to pay their mortgages, rather than the other way around). And, crucially, there's only so much of it – as Mark Twain put it, "They're not making it anymore."

The supply is doubly fixed, given that each parcel of land occupies a unique location. It's often observed that Australia has an abundance of land. But *well-located* land – near jobs, public transport, services and amenities – is limited. This, of course, is where most people want to live.

This is a bigger challenge in Australia than elsewhere. Australia has unusually high population growth – only one other country in the developed world has such consistently high growth. Also unusually, Australians are highly concentrated in a few large, low-density cities. Between them, Melbourne, Sydney and Brisbane house half the population, the majority living in low-density areas between the CBDs and fringe greenfield developments.

This combination of high population growth and an unusual urban settlement pattern makes well-located urban land much scarcer in Australia than elsewhere. And when a good is scarce, we can expect its value to increase. In our white paper *What Drives Australian House Prices Over the Long Term*, we have calculated that, driven by land value, residential property now constitutes almost half of Australia's total national assets.

So while many point the finger at various government policies or inaction as the principal problem, we think the problems are fundamentally structural, rooted in the role of land values. As such, no simple change in government policy can solve them. Given how hard it is for governments to act in this area, that is probably just as well.

On a parenthetical note, it is essential to distinguish between land value and building value. While buildings typically depreciate over time (as wear and tear erode their value, and desirability decreases relative to newer buildings), land, especially well-located land, appreciates due to its limited and scarce nature. Houses and other detached dwellings typically have the major proportion of their value consisting of land value, while high-density apartments typically have a low proportion. This distinction contributes to the varied growth profiles of different property types, with detached dwellings exhibiting the strongest growth, and higher-density apartments typically experiencing the lowest.

What to do? We think the creation of an Australian Housing Fund industry is the real solution.

To have any chance of working at the scale required, solutions need to run with the economics of the Australian property market, rather than against them. The role of land value described above makes Australia a high capital-growth residential property market. It is also, therefore, a lower-yield market, unlike, for example, the US residential property market, which in the main is characterised by higher yields. This means that overseas solutions, such as Build to Rent, which rely on good yields for their returns to investors, run counter to the economics of the Australian property market and are likely not to be attractive enough to make a significant difference.

But a high-growth market also constitutes an opportunity. At the moment, there are only two ways to benefit from the high capital growth available in Australia: owner occupation, and direct property investment through being a landlord. At the same time, high house prices relative to incomes make deposits ever harder to save, locking too many people out of home ownership. They are then stuck in a poorly performing private rental system which works for neither renters nor landlords (the former get poor tenure security and a poor experience, while the latter get poor average returns along with management and maintenance headaches).

The capital growth available in Australia's housing market – driven by our population growth and settlement structure – means that large amounts of private capital could be mobilised to help solve these problems. In *Mobilising Private Capital for Housing Solutions*, we argue that a Housing Fund industry could be put to work by using investors' money to solve two enormous challenges: to help people into home ownership through shared equity; and to give renters security of tenure and a better experience.

Shared-equity models can ease Australia's housing affordability crisis by allowing homebuyers to purchase property with lower savings for a deposit in exchange for giving some of their home's equity or capital growth to a third party. Housing funds would provide the capital for shared-equity providers to co-invest with eligible homebuyers. Governments are now offering shared equity in most jurisdictions but we will need private capital to meet needs that are an order of magnitude bigger than governments can fund.

This is particularly relevant for first homebuyers or those who have difficulty saving for the large deposit needed to purchase a home, including those who do not have access to financial assistance from the Bank of Mum and Dad.

Home ownership, even with a mortgage, is the best form of housing security in Australia, with no risk of residency being terminated by a landlord, and numerous protections from banks and governments to help financially at-risk households avoid foreclosure. Home owners also experience a higher quality of experience than renters, facing few restrictions around alterations or renovations, and aren't subject to inspections, lease contract renewals or disrespectful treatment by poor property managers.

For those who cannot or do not want to own, housing funds would also invest in owning and managing large portfolios of long-term rental properties – a model long established in mainland Europe. These would provide tenants with a security of tenure not currently available in the private rental market, along with a significantly better renting experience. Housing funds could further differentiate themselves by giving tenants guarantees relating to safety, autonomy, flexibility and dignity. Multi-year rental agreements, interior alterations, maintenance request guarantees, high minimum standards on heating and cooling, energy retrofitting and minimum energy-efficiency standards would all be in the interests of the providers as well as tenants. Governments should ensure that the industry is regulated so that only reputable providers are able to operate – lessons should be learnt from the United States, where there is both good and bad provision.

It should be noted that current land tax policy represents a significant barrier to the development of institutional ownership in Australia. Other than in the ACT, under current settings the more land that individuals and corporations own, the higher their land tax rates. Since providers of affordable housing, who rent at a discount to the market, are exempt from land tax, the only current pathway for institutional ownership is as affordable housing providers. This is good for the provision of below-market rentals but means that households in the private rental system would not be able to access the tenure security and improved experience that institutional ownership would make possible.

The almost $10-trillion residential housing market and the growing scale of our housing crises mean that governments alone will never be able to fix them. The capital growth in Australian housing alone is roughly equal in size to the entire federal budget. But there could be a scalable solution through mobilising private capital.

The federal government recently announced a major push to work with superannuation funds to engage with Australian housing, as they currently have very little exposure to Australian residential property despite their substantial size and the magnitude of the asset class. Indeed, when discussing private investment in Australia, most of the discussion, and certainly most policy emphasis, is focused on institutional investors – notably large superannuation funds.

A much larger source of capital lies with landlords, where two and a half million individual property investors between them have over $2 trillion invested in over a quarter of Australia's residential property market (and, in contrast to superannuation funds, have already chosen the asset class). And, because much of this capital is generating poor returns alongside daily problems for both landlords and renters, it is a capital pool that is ripe for redeployment for better housing outcomes. Corporate, family office and high-net-worth individuals also have an important role to play, particularly in seeding demonstration funds.

Our inspiration for these funds is the creation, forty years ago, of Australia's superannuation funds, which have revolutionised our post-work lives. The role of superannuation funds is to provide secure dignified retirement. Given the opportunity, housing funds could become the architects of secure dignified housing.

Evan Thornley & Jane-Frances Kelly

THE GREAT DIVIDE

Response to Correspondence

Alan Kohler

Tackling Australia's housing mess in a Quarterly Essay was a daunting task, partly because it's a big, complicated mess, but also because everyone has a firm opinion on the subject and a lot of smart people have spent their lives studying it, and I'm not one of them. But the responses to the essay have been plentiful, informative and gratifying, including the ones from those who weren't impressed with what I had written; as always, you learn more from those who disagree with you than those who agree. I'm grateful for all of them.

Brendan Coates and Joey Maloney at the Grattan Institute didn't like my suggestion of fast trains to open up regional areas for viable commuting to the city, which they called an "unfortunate misfire" and Peter Tulip thought I overemphasised the impact of tax concessions. I want to deal in detail with each of these two responses because I learnt from them, and they get to the heart of the problem – and the solutions.

Brendan and Joey think I too easily dismissed the potential for densifying the suburbs – that is, building more medium-density housing in good locations that use existing infrastructure. They tell us that, going into the pandemic, Australia had 400 homes per 1000 people, among the least amount of housing stock per person in the developed world, and we have some of the least dense cities. The reason is simple, they say: the processes that dictate what gets built where are hugely biased against change.

The answer, they assert, is equally simple: "If the problem is not enough homes in established suburbs, surely any meaningful solution must involve building more homes in said suburbs?"

"Kohler misses the moment," they write. "The political mood is changing. There is a growing groundswell of support for more density, and a growing awareness of the costs of locking up vast tracts of our cities from development."

They are dead right that I've missed that. If there is a groundswell of support for more density, it has passed me by, which is clearly a failure on my part.

Brendan and Joey say that I am unduly pessimistic, and they are also dead right that I'm pessimistic – about the capacity of Australian politics to deliver difficult solutions about anything, especially denser housing. Unduly so, as they assert? Time will tell. I really hope the men from Grattan are right and I'm wrong, because it's quite true that "denser cities are more efficient cities," and that by far the simplest solution to the shortage of housing and high prices would be more medium-density housing close to the city.

To drive home my misfire, Mark Walker persuasively explains the difficulties of fast trains:

> It is the convoluted, contour-following nature of the original nineteenth-century track alignment that still largely dictates the speed of trains today. To speed them up, we need to spend big on upgrading the actual line of rail – the embankments, viaducts and cuttings on which the rails are laid … The problem is centrifugal force. The faster a train travels, the gentler must be the bends in the track, or the engines and carriages can tip up, and tip over.

So that seals it: fast trains are too expensive and they won't be needed because the NIMBYs are in retreat. What I wrote in the essay is wrong, it seems, and I couldn't be happier about that.

Peter Tulip's complaint is that I put too much weight on the impact of negative gearing and the capital gains tax discount introduced in 1999 – any weight at all, in fact. "There is no credible research supporting this claim," he writes.

When I began this project, I decided to investigate and explain the housing problem in three steps: first, what happened to house prices; second, what the effect on Australia and its citizens has been; and third, when it happened. I thought the "when" would help explain the "why," and all these things together would provide the solutions. The "when," I thought, was evident from the two charts towards the front of the essay of house prices against both incomes and GDP. It obviously happened in 2000.

I admire Peter's work and his expertise, and he says I should have used a logarithmic (log) scale, which would have told a different story: that "an acceleration can be seen [after 2000], but it is not dramatic and it begins before the tax change."

Log scales are used to show exponential curves because they don't fit on a graph. I'm not sure why a log scale is needed for house prices. Peter includes a log-scale chart of house prices in his response, which he says shows that house prices started rising before 2000. Well, looking at his chart, it's clear that prices were broadly flat from 1972 to 1987, jumped sharply between 1987 and 1990, which was the rise "before the tax change" that Peter talks about, were flat again for ten years, and then from 2000 rose rapidly and inexorably for more than twenty years to the present day.

I'm sorry, but I reckon that rise in Peter's log-scale graph is dramatic, and I just don't accept that the jump in prices in the late 1980s – which was the property bubble and bust that produced the 1991 recession – rules out the tax reforms of 1999 as an important cause of rising house prices. If anything, Peter's chart reinforces the point, even without including household incomes or GDP.

Graphs aside, house prices increased at 3 per cent per annum before 2000, the same rate as income, and 6 per cent after 2000, double the rate of income. So I stand by the proposition that the psychological effect of halving the capital gains tax with pre-existing negative gearing deductions had a big impact on demand for houses, and that removing those tax concessions must be an important part of dealing with housing affordability.

But I appreciated the generous efforts of Peter, Brendan and Joey to set me straight, and of course the kind words of many others, including those responses that couldn't be printed for space reasons. I particularly valued Judith Brett's historical insights, Nicole Haddow's millennial viewpoint and Nicholas Reece's local council perspective.

The process of researching this subject and then engaging with responses to my essay has confirmed that this is a subject about which a lot of people have been thinking deeply and expertly for a long time, and Australia is well served by them. It's just a pity they are not listened to more. We are less well served by the politicians and bureaucrats whose job it is to do something about it.

Alan Kohler

Lech Blaine is the author of the memoir *Car Crash* and the Quarterly Essay *Top Blokes*. He is the 2023 Charles Perkins Centre writer in residence. His writing has appeared in *Good Weekend*, *Griffith Review*, *The Guardian* and *The Monthly*.

Judith Brett is emeritus professor of politics at La Trobe University. A former editor of *Meanjin* and columnist for *The Age*, she won the National Biography Award in 2018 for *The Enigmatic Mr Deakin*. She is the author of four Quarterly Essays.

Brendan Coates is the Economic Policy Program Director at the Grattan Institute.

Saul Eslake is an economist, speaker and Vice Chancellor's Fellow at the University of Tasmania. He is a member of the panel of expert advisers to Australia's Parliamentary Budget Office.

Nicole Haddow is a Victoria-based journalist and the author of *Smashed Avocado: How I cracked the property market and you can too* and *The Ethical Investor*. She was the executive property writer for the *Australian Financial Review*.

Jane-Frances Kelly is Head of Strategy and Insights at LongView. She is co-author of *City Limits: Why Australia's cities are broken and how we can fix them*.

Alan Kohler is finance presenter on *ABC News* and a columnist for *The New Daily*. A former editor of *The Age* and the *Australian Financial Review*, he founded the *Eureka Report* and has written for *The Australian*, the *AFR*, *The Age* and *The Sydney Morning Herald*. His books include *It's Your Money*.

Peter Mares writes about housing and other public policy issues for *Inside Story* and is the author of *No Place Like Home: Repairing Australia's housing crisis*. He is adjunct senior research fellow at Monash University's School of Meda, Film and Journalism and a fellow at the Centre for Policy Development.

Joey Moloney is a deputy program director at the Grattan Institute.

Nicholas Reece is the deputy lord mayor of the City of Melbourne and leads the City Planning Portfolio. He is also a principal fellow at the Melbourne School of Government at the University of Melbourne.

Stephen Smith is an economist and partner at Deloitte Access Economics. The views expressed here are his own and do not necessarily represent the views of Deloitte Australia.

Evan Thornley is a social entrepreneur, philanthropist, impact investor and co-founder and executive chair of LongView.

Peter Tulip is chief economist at the Centre for Independent Studies. He previously worked at the Reserve Bank of Australia and the US Federal Reserve. He has written several research papers on Australian housing policy.

Joseph Walker is an Emergent Ventures winner and host of *The Joe Walker Podcast*. His background is in technology start-ups, most recently as director of operations at Y Combinator–backed Forage.

Mark Walker is a writer, journalist and former manager with a major rail construction and maintenance contractor.

Pete Wargent is a financial and housing market analyst and a former director at Deloitte. He is the author of *Get a Financial Grip: A simple plan for financial freedom* and other books.

WANT THE LATEST FROM QUARTERLY ESSAY?

Subscribe to the Friends of Quarterly Essay email newsletter to share in news, updates, events and special offers.

quarterlyessay.com.au/signup

QUARTERLY ESSAY BACK ISSUES

- ☐ **QE 1** ($27.99) Robert Manne *In Denial*
- ☐ **QE 2** ($27.99) John Birmingham *Appeasing Jakarta*
- ☐ **QE 3** ($27.99) Guy Rundle *The Opportunist*
- ☐ **QE 4** ($27.99) Don Watson *Rabbit Syndrome*
- ☐ **QE 5** ($27.99) Mungo MacCallum *Girt By Sea*
- ☐ **QE 6** ($27.99) John Button *Beyond Belief*
- ☐ **QE 7** ($27.99) John Martinkus *Paradise Betrayed*
- **QE 8** Amanda Lohrey *Groundswell* OUT OF STOCK
- ☐ **QE 9** ($27.99) Tim Flannery *Beautiful Lies*
- ☐ **QE 10** ($27.99) Gideon Haigh *Bad Company*
- ☐ **QE 11** ($27.99) Germaine Greer *Whitefella Jump Up*
- ☐ **QE 12** ($27.99) David Malouf *Made in England*
- ☐ **QE 13** ($27.99) Robert Manne with David Corlett *Sending Them Home*
- ☐ **QE 14** ($27.99) Paul McGeough *Mission Impossible*
- ☐ **QE 15** ($27.99) Margaret Simons *Latham's World*
- ☐ **QE 16** ($27.99) Raimond Gaita *Breach of Trust*
- ☐ **QE 17** ($27.99) John Hirst *'Kangaroo Court'*
- ☐ **QE 18** ($27.99) Gail Bell *The Worried Well*
- ☐ **QE 19** ($27.99) Judith Brett *Relaxed & Comfortable*
- ☐ **QE 20** ($27.99) John Birmingham *A Time for War*
- ☐ **QE 21** ($27.99) Clive Hamilton *What's Left?*
- ☐ **QE 22** ($27.99) Amanda Lohrey *Voting for Jesus*
- ☐ **QE 23** ($27.99) Inga Clendinnen *The History Question*
- ☐ **QE 24** ($27.99) Robyn Davidson *No Fixed Address*
- ☐ **QE 25** ($27.99) Peter Hartcher *Bipolar Nation*
- ☐ **QE 26** ($27.99) David Marr *His Master's Voice*
- ☐ **QE 27** ($27.99) Ian Lowe *Reaction Time*
- ☐ **QE 28** ($27.99) Judith Brett *Exit Right*
- ☐ **QE 29** ($27.99) Anne Manne *Love & Money*
- ☐ **QE 30** ($27.99) Paul Toohey *Last Drinks*
- ☐ **QE 31** ($27.99) Tim Flannery *Now or Never*
- ☐ **QE 32** ($27.99) Kate Jennings *American Revolution*
- ☐ **QE 33** ($27.99) Guy Pearse *Quarry Vision*
- ☐ **QE 34** ($27.99) Annabel Crabb *Stop at Nothing*
- ☐ **QE 35** ($27.99) Noel Pearson *Radical Hope*
- ☐ **QE 36** ($27.99) Mungo MacCallum *Australian Story*
- ☐ **QE 37** ($27.99) Waleed Aly *What's Right?*
- ☐ **QE 38** ($27.99) David Marr *Power Trip*
- ☐ **QE 39** ($27.99) Hugh White *Power Shift*
- ☐ **QE 40** ($27.99) George Megalogenis *Trivial Pursuit*
- ☐ **QE 41** ($27.99) David Malouf *The Happy Life*
- ☐ **QE 42** ($27.99) Judith Brett *Fair Share*
- ☐ **QE 43** ($27.99) Robert Manne *Bad News*
- ☐ **QE 44** ($27.99) Andrew Charlton *Man-Made World*
- ☐ **QE 45** ($27.99) Anna Krien *Us and Them*
- ☐ **QE 46** ($27.99) Laura Tingle *Great Expectations*
- ☐ **QE 47** ($27.99) David Marr *Political Animal*
- ☐ **QE 48** ($27.99) Tim Flannery *After the Future*
- ☐ **QE 49** ($27.99) Mark Latham *Not Dead Yet*
- ☐ **QE 50** ($27.99) Anna Goldsworthy *Unfinished Business*
- ☐ **QE 51** ($27.99) David Marr *The Prince*
- ☐ **QE 52** ($27.99) Linda Jaivin *Found in Translation*
- ☐ **QE 53** ($27.99) Paul Toohey *That Sinking Feeling*
- ☐ **QE 54** ($27.99) Andrew Charlton *Dragon's Tail*
- ☐ **QE 55** ($27.99) Noel Pearson *A Rightful Place*
- ☐ **QE 56** ($27.99) Guy Rundle *Clivosaurus*
- ☐ **QE 57** ($27.99) Karen Hitchcock *Dear Life*
- ☐ **QE 58** ($27.99) David Kilcullen *Blood Year*
- ☐ **QE 59** ($27.99) David Marr *Faction Man*
- ☐ **QE 60** ($27.99) Laura Tingle *Political Amnesia*
- ☐ **QE 61** ($27.99) George Megalogenis *Balancing Act*
- ☐ **QE 62** ($27.99) James Brown *Firing Line*
- ☐ **QE 63** ($27.99) Don Watson *Enemy Within*
- ☐ **QE 64** ($27.99) Stan Grant *The Australian Dream*
- ☐ **QE 65** ($27.99) David Marr *The White Queen*
- ☐ **QE 66** ($27.99) Anna Krien *The Long Goodbye*
- ☐ **QE 67** ($27.99) Benjamin Law *Moral Panic 101*
- ☐ **QE 68** ($27.99) Hugh White *Without America*
- ☐ **QE 69** ($27.99) Mark McKenna *Moment of Truth*
- ☐ **QE 70** ($27.99) Richard Denniss *Dead Right*
- ☐ **QE 71** ($27.99) Laura Tingle *Follow the Leader*
- ☐ **QE 72** ($27.99) Sebastian Smee *Net Loss*
- ☐ **QE 73** ($27.99) Rebecca Huntley *Australia Fair*
- ☐ **QE 74** ($27.99) Erik Jensen *The Prosperity Gospel*
- ☐ **QE 75** ($27.99) Annabel Crabb *Men at Work*
- ☐ **QE 76** ($27.99) Peter Hartcher *Red Flag*
- ☐ **QE 77** ($27.99) Margaret Simons *Cry Me a River*
- ☐ **QE 78** ($27.99) Judith Brett *The Coal Curse*
- ☐ **QE 79** ($27.99) Katharine Murphy *The End of Certainty*
- ☐ **QE 80** ($27.99) Laura Tingle *The High Road*
- ☐ **QE 81** ($27.99) Alan Finkel *Getting to Zero*
- ☐ **QE 82** ($27.99) George Megalogenis *Exit Strategy*
- ☐ **QE 83** ($27.99) Lech Blaine *Top Blokes*
- ☐ **QE 84** ($27.99) Jess Hill *The Reckoning*
- ☐ **QE 85** ($27.99) Sarah Krasnostein *Not Waving, Drowning*
- ☐ **QE 86** ($27.99) Hugh White *Sleepwalk to War*
- ☐ **QE 87** ($27.99) Waleed Aly & Scott Stephens *Uncivil Wars*
- ☐ **QE 88** ($27.99) Katharine Murphy *Lone Wolf*
- ☐ **QE 89** ($27.99) Saul Griffith *The Wires That Bind*
- ☐ **QE 90** ($27.99) Megan Davis *Voice of Reason*
- ☐ **QE 91** ($27.99) Micheline Lee *Lifeboat*
- ☐ **QE 92** ($27.99) Alan Kohler *The Great Divide*

Prices include GST, postage and handling within Australia. Please include this form with delivery and payment details overleaf.
Back issues also available as ebooks from ebook retailers.